POEMS IN RETROSPECT
A SELECTION

By Stephen Oliver

Henwise (1975)

& interviews (1978)

Autumn Songs (1978)

Letter To James K. Baxter (1980)

Earthbound Mirrors (1984)

Guardians, Not Angels (1993)

Islands of Wilderness—A Romance (1996)

Unmanned (1999)

Election Year Blues (1999)

Night of Warehouses: Poems 1978-2000 (2001)

Deadly Pollen (2003)

Ballads, Satire & Salt—A Book of Diversions (2003)

Either Side The Horizon (2005)

Parable of The Sea Sponge (2007)

Harmonic (2008)

Apocrypha (2010)

Intercolonial (2013)

Gone: Satirical Poems: New & Selected (2016)

Luxembourg (2018)

Heroides/15 Sonnets (2020)

The Song of Globule/80 Sonnets (2020)

Cranial Bunker (2023)

Prose

Unposted, Autumn Leaves/A Memoir In Essays (2021)

POEMS IN RETROSPECT

A SELECTION

STEPHEN OLIVER

GP
GREYWACKE PRESS
Lat. 25°/50° South. Long. 145°/180° East

First published 2025

Greywacke Press
9 Lynch St
Hughes
ACT 2605
Australia
reid1801@bigpond.com
greywackepress@gmail.com

Oliver, Stephen 1950-
Title: Poems In Retrospect: *A Selection*
ISBN   978-0-646-89314-3

Cover design composed by Stephen Oliver
Cover layout, Tina Wilson, One Tentacle Publishing, Australia
Affinity formatting, John Denny, Puriri Press, NZ

Front cover, untitled watercolour by Frank Wright,
1860-1923, English born artist, emigrated to NZ in 1885

A catalogue record for this book is available from the
National Library of Australia

© Stephen Oliver

Acknowledgements

Many of these poems are revised and taken from the following collections:

Henwise, Hawk Press, Taylors Mistake, Christchurch 1975; *& interviews*, Horizontal Press, Auckland 1978; *Autumn Songs*, Horizontal Press, Auckland 1978; *Earthbound Mirrors*, Horizontal Press, Auckland 1984; *Guardians, Not Angels*, Hazard Press, Christchurch 1993; *Islands of Wilderness—A Romance* [in] *The Wild Life*, ed., Judith Rodriguez, Penguin Books, Australia 1996; *Unmanned*, HeadworX, Wellington 1999; *Night of Warehouses: Poems 1978-2000*, HeadworX, Wellington 2001; *Ballads, Satire & Salt: A Book of Diversions* (illust. by Matt Ottley), Greywacke Press, Sydney 2003; *Deadly Pollen*, Word Riot Press, Middletown/NJ, USA 2003; *Either Side The Horizon*, Titus Books, Auckland 2005; *Harmonic*, IP, Brisbane 2008; *Intercolonial*, Puriri Press, Auckland 2013; *GONE: Satirical Poems: New & Selected* (illust. by Matt Ottley), Greywacke Press, Canberra 2016; *Luxembourg*, Greywacke Press, Canberra 2018; *The Song of Globule: 80 Sonnets*, Greywacke Press, Canberra 2020; *Cranial Bunker*, Greywacke Press, Canberra 2023.

Autumn Songs, Horizontal Press, Auckland 1978, though published as a separate chapbook properly belongs to *& interviews* and is therefore incorporated into that poem.

Something In The Air, a 35 mm film short based on the poem taken from the collection, *Earthbound Mirrors* (1984), recorded by the author at Mascot Studios Auckland to an original music score by the Auckland jazz musician, Bob Jackson, and directed and produced by Allan MacGillivray & Stephen Oliver. The film first screened at the *Auckland International Film Festival 1986*. Screened at the *Roma Theatre, Sydney*, dist. CEL 1987; the sound track of the movie uploaded onto SoundCloud along with many other poems recorded by the author.

The Find, taken from *Night of Warehouses: Poems 1978-2000* (2001), read by the author Stephen Oliver in a 16 mm film, directed by Donavan Gabrielsen & Emma Farry (2009). Converted to a digital, video poem now available on YouTube.

The poems, *Something In The Air*, *7.5 On The Richter Scale*, *Mosaic*, *Black Concentrations*, *Earthbound Mirrors*, *Song of Gravity*, *The Find*, recorded by the author at Mandrill Studios and released through Ode Records: *Earthbound Mirrors, Stephen Oliver*, (audio cassette) Auckland 1984.

The following poems feature on the KING HIT CD—written & read by Stephen Oliver to original music by Matt Ottley. ID Brisbane, Australia 2007; Nos: 32, 78 from *Islands of Wilderness—A Romance* sung by Hester Hannah, *The Grey Glas Song* (Willy McElroy on the bodhran), *Brady's Grave, Braidwood, Oldest Pine, Emblem For Dead Youth, The Woolshed, Letter To An Astronomer, Hania, Gaudeamus Igitur, Ballad of Miss Goodbar, A Simple Tale*—these last two poems produced and recorded by the author as video poems on YouTube.

No 47 from *Islands of Wilderness—A Romance*, translated into German by Rudi Krausmann, Austrian born Australian playwright and poet (1933-2019), subsequently appeared in *Literatur und Kritik* (Austria). *Streets of Kiev* in the original English (Russian translation by Max Nemtsov), subsequently published in *East West Literary Forum*, New York.

The Song of Globule: 80 Sonnets No: 80: *follow the rails*—regarding the closing line, 'the last train out of Sydney's almost gone.' The original Cold Chisel *Khe Sanh* lyric reads 'plane' not 'train'. I adopted 'train' as it endorses the sonnet content.

Deadly Pollen (2003), the complete poem translated into Spanish (*Polen Mortal*) by the Chilean poet, Sergio Badilla Castillo, with thanks to Roger Hickin of Cold Hub Press, Lyttelton NZ for arranging this translation, and published in the Spanish language magazine, *Nagari*, Vol 7 July, USA 2015.

Contents

'The windlasses haul down the dry hulls seaward'
—*Horace*: Odes: Book 1: IV

POEMS IN RETROSPECT
A SELECTION

HENWISE

The Fall　　　i

The individual Hen
moves pausefully at dawn
breaking off bits of the night
from her beak

and preening, Hen
treats the separate quill
as barometer, tapping the feather
for flicker of beauty.

The wing is a crab
freezing hard the tendons which
set fowl in the leafless
primordial skies

where caws
no man heard from throats
leathered and reptilian, creatures
fated with monstrosity
suffering the sin
of an abrupt and too quick
yeasted evolution. When earth went
prim and proper

its forests and fronds
not as grotesque and frightful
such creatures to the unspiked
canopies of green

rolled to their finality, rounded to a ball
of feather. As things suppose their order
they fall unperched.

This Hen knows—
with feathers atremble,
woodblock hollowed with
the stain of blood;
the brain alarmed
at the call of the housewife's pot

and the wars,
games for the small fry,
as all the while, Rooster
makes much ado of morning
red cactus bristling
on the skull, he flushes
to give the worm time muster.

Yet the days
that were happy for lice
in the warm compress
at play in the downy dark
of mother Hen's nest
are beaten by the beak
of a muffled chirper—

and the body,
it fills out tight as a glove
as the poult takes grip
on the life habit
to scratch out what it can
or those who can't,
the chick pursues the
kill at cockcrow.

Abstraction   iv

Then the eye snaps all the
things moving, moving faster—
oiling the shuttered eye lens
objects slip into sight
and flash the nerve ends

to drag the brain into flight
which rends, is bending
Hen from the terrain's grip
wings useless as lead

but if action's quick enough
all's awhirl and amiss,
for Hen to soar by a wish
is so many images
faltering—in wind.

What Neighbour Does And Thinks   v

Strong as hemp rope
on rafter arch and fencepost,
twisting like devil rain, stoat
tightens on the undone chicken.

Stoat inches like a damp fuse
his brain kindled to pick
through the ruins of bone tissue
and clenches and sound proofs

                the tiniest scream.

Daytime is a while away
of hours, and maybe fierce hopes
and a deal of sleep as if
by rote, waking to the blank desire

the black mass of the kill.
Stoat eases from the tubers and fern
dragging no grudge from the night ago,
though driven with a foodful habit

his thought is lean.

Other Contenders   vi

A yelp wrapped in fur shifts
at dawn about coop and perch
willed to pad jaws with quill
and pinpricked meat

the Hen eye
catches the soft pawed doom
of dog packing
to a jury of death

over the waiting Hen.
Night like a collar
loosens the moon among leaves
and cusps Hen like a shell.

A sponge athrob with blood
hides grotesque under wraps
of vein, plotting to expand
its world at a crack—

and when the deed is cut
chicken grows fat on the 'I am'
of a brave new liveliness,
shadowed under the spur of

As It Is   xi

Black is moss and nugget like
                under clumps of grass
as though doors to cave retreats
                awaited, not to be
unlocked by the Hen's foraging
                set upon higher things.

An hour is weeded from minutes
                with clocked cunning
leaving a trap of time behind
                and filling the flesh
with ache—no chance to escape
                from a primitive wish.

Earth has dropped with a stamp
                around the wishful Hen
as the yearly seasons pull free
                a carbon dated memory
waking Hen hateful when the day's
                to the face of dark.

Repose   xii

The copper banks   are
                                whipped with
abandoned talons
                needles, fossils in the

earsofwind   and
                                ditchways.
Autumn: atomic season

        of
                moulting

as old skin

lift   flags of surrender;

        drabness—
                a dark box over
                        the fowl run.

Autumn occasions
                whining in the throat

astheneckshuts
                in the shoulders
forWarmth.

Autumn, and the breath   gathers like
                burntsnow

                and leaves like marshlands
sweat in orchards,   and
                        creatures thinking on
l o s s   are

                gregarious.

Winter Is Heartfelt   xiii

Hugely,
        this petrol stain
loops the moon to cloud

                (rain is tossed)

        to white straw
reset is the timing and Hen
moves to her shed of branch.

Oil proofed

           as canvas Hen
jerked the quill from flesh
              (blood is drugged)

an asbestos sky takes
up winter Hen proposes leaves
to twigs kindled for wetness.

Blood Wedding   xv

The neck has reddened to a lip,
          Rooster bolted, fixes as a dart
                      and submission:

Hen's belly hovers upon dust
          his wings hydrofoil—*she* cushions

and the protest whirrs distant as
              a spectator and circles.

These twin lusts incorporate stillness
and the scream comes home again

drained of its echo—resides in the throat—
around and about, the landmarks,
          seated tight as an audience
over the pulled Hen.

Presage Of Dust   xvii

This fabled bird
queries the fanfare of dust
bounding on air and sun,
herald of aeons said and done.
The Hen eye

marvels at
the sun's aeronautics
and scans the dust
catching in the horde, withered
breath of ancient deaths:

the many considerations of dust
mass to evil flower
as the flights of so much
soul stuff—migratory flocks
of the dead.

Song   xviii

Say here was resurrection
that came into the trees
adding physique to the leaves
that there was no glory in it
simple birds rising like dust
out of the hard mixed day
before the stars settled down
like wax onto the sky.

Say here was the time
that bird mindful of danger
vowed unto the nightly odour
whole families for the foliage
sprung to branches like a wedge
beyond reach of an enemy's scorn
holding together much as a rhyme
before dawn broke that pledge.

By Invitation Only   xix

The gap widens.
              Green bile retches through earth
          and at one gasp—daybreak!
                  Quicksilver lodged
          in the chest of night
                  and the sun turns the land
                      on its spit.

The light fattens.
              There is movement abroad
          and instinct reclaims
                  the body
                      phlegmatic
          the species of Hen
                  assemble for roll call by order.

Assembly Of Fowls   xx

Cockerel thought this day had come the
'spiked heel as chariot'
the usual rabble at this time and Hen with
whetted appetite threshed wings.

Rooster saw broth boil 'the game's up'
          and took his ration first
called by number from Hen to poult the rank
          and file fed.

Cockerel was last, took his course
          and broke rank
while the pullets flurried propaganda:
          'the egg and the curse'.

Thus the claim of Rooster's flight
        broken with age
he bandied his defences an empire crumbled
        in this throat and he grounded.

16.   */still life*

The window falls down to earth that is certain   imperturbable
the window flows in gravity

a fly fixed there would take a hundred years to shift its
                    length on the glass tide

outside I view the world as a hall of mirrors
day by days the land distorts

the wind is buckled / the putty sound of skin stretched /
the turning of the head

tomorrow the clouds I hang neatly as curtains.

21.   */answers*

There are of course, numerous combinations …
my cells regard but don't decide against *your* sex.

I argue with my hormones
as the old tyranny exerts, again, you upon me.

Who gathers about you now?
I cannot hear your breath.

Even before your cells met in conference
to spill warmth one into the other

the brute impact felled you
knocked whole zones of flesh into silence.

You do not know it, now
that absolute rejection flows smoothly through you.

34.   /*incident*

Birds knew   (the wait   then the second shock)

I know it
that in the space of one morning / a space /

the macrocarpa toppled to the next door paddock
because we heard it   the land rattled

as at low level the trunk was cut

             we saw the whole operation

through our casement windows that frame   now
more open air.

45.   /*sketches*

Before the winds—
             those trumpets!

The absolute length of the wall dropped
that is, the sea fell: flat
                              /

lettering, graffito   (not words)
figures, hieroglyph   the unexplained billboard

lay down with much noise onto the land
                  and is still falling.

I do not ask you to match
your parenthesis of understanding

against that of the sea   still falling
before those trumpets—it is   inconclusive.

autumn songs

1.   */the gathering*

In this month   the unexpected
partitions of light emerge;

the airy carpentry of autumn.

Campfires burn on the harbour
(rather) the funnels of ships

offering foreign smoke before
the flat accents of the city line

and the grey flank of Rangitoto.

The entire aggression of growth
enters into the cul-de-sac.   Of leaf.

3.   /*the flight*

Grapeshot of blackbird
get there before the stars do,

Black Concentrations!

So the fabric loosens
and the mesh of the centre is diffuse

(allows mist through).

Then, as they are about to settle
I see them scuffing the inches

off next season's spring.
Over the rise and fall of the tree line

such Black Concentrations!

10.   /*the direction*

The gathering of the cloud, the wind,
the rainstorm.

The ringing of the doorbell, the house search,
the arrest.

The sky constantly invaded
and pretty, delicate elements are led away

howling.

The fine birds that make up our blood,
I count them

the red and white flocks flittering through
on the migratory path,

the blue tunnels, forever hidden by their settling.

Except in this,
an observation that the blood flows out of me

where, perhaps, you thought me rock?

Everything is an even stress between us;
I lope a vowel past you   unknowingly.

12.   */the orchardist*

The smell of largeness, of breath,
white destinations of rain

lift over the glass
these fragmented molecules:

the dizziness of a too upright man.

How the motes before his eyes
catch at the skeins of pride

lungs big as a cloud—
who will take anything in his stride;

an obstacle course played in a
set of rhymes.

Purple leaves at his soles.

epilogue

The grey overcoat of the sky flung open!
A hundred buttons threaded with rain

wrapped about itself and as suddenly—stopped.
The air disintegrated, or perhaps that's too neat?

It becomes harder and harder to people
these lines

to lay them flat as on a slab of ice.
With a gunshot I could evoke a crowd

but I don't wish that either. I am
a white-coated official hemmed within,

completely attendant on the Brueghel noises
of the mob—
                    wrapped about itself.

These lines then, are hurdles
they are poles to bruise the shins of the rabble.

The tongue that troubles
the top of the mouth
                    is a bird flight

that takes me back to initial ancestors
who coupled together in rhyme

who created the memory of me
that takes me back   *that* turns me back.

I would like to say I am vintage
of all which consumes me—that I

would like to have said a lot of things
though have not scanned these yet.

Meanwhile, across the light
my shadow behind me   behind me walks out.

The moment drops as though deadwood
and there is light slipping from it

and there is a breath of wind,
this wind that parts wooden mobiles.

The bleep of lie detectors
on the branches

on the sonic trees
pressed out under an overpass

which takes a left hand turn
into dusk—

from these birds piled high along the plane trees.

For them and me the same repetition
the simple image of the hour to take refuge in.

If you wish,
I am making bricks out of air for them and me.

All it takes is for one bird to escape
one wing to drop like a half-moon

and then the thing is undone
as a girl who walks the middle of the street

at night. Who veers neither left nor right.
The air has gone clear.

Your whisper is a heated flat iron
pressed to my ear

clear as the visibility of day. Clear as that.
Sounds are flying night blind

as though a playground
or the vocals of it had assembled on the air.

I hear
that your voice takes too much of my vision

and crowds me in.
I elaborate—and why I make bricks out of air.

EARTHBOUND MIRRORS

SOMETHING IN THE AIR

Auckland you big arsehole,
ah, soul is what the man meant, what you lack

on this pock/baked earth scraped from the barren uteri of
The Seven Dead Ones.

But that don't matter a scrap
as you ease your carcass into the breech of summer

into the season of reprieve and airy flocculence.
It is summer.

Summertime, and the intersecting motorways
sparkle with loads of tinsel that dissolve and bubble

through long distances of heat.
There is something in the air,

and it is not that coruscating light
which burns down through the fluffy elements

that drift and break against the cold sides of the sky.
An unique breed here in Wood Street, in Wood Street,

which leads onto a home (in Elizabeth Street)
for them other citizens, there without fortune

have had (it) their souls slammed in the door of Auckland.

You would think it broke them, yes, their backs
that they carry so much weight

to & fro Wood Street they go

they carry the imaginary golden key to this city on backs
bowed   it breaks them   *them's the breaks buddy*.

To & fro Wood Street they go
bearing that weight, and I wonder

whether them broken backs feel it too,

they could be sniffing the air?

•• ••

'O the Gulf
opens out a chest bare as Sir Dove-Myer Robinson
heaving

in the morning
light shapes up for another day of commercial
wham bam

(thank you ma'am)
O thank you for turning out and already one of them
days

where cloud
has discounted some of the brightness off the hours
(the weatherman tells us)

and nose sense
tells me that here we've got a ring / ding / ding /
of a queen city.'

And only then is the air tight with warning.

•• ••

This is a poem and place of asides.

This is a town of asides; public ground has been set aside
for:

public walks have been set aside
for:

street corners have been set aside
for:
recreational purposes and pick/ups.

Victoria Park is a green depth swimming under an overpass

and the heavy pollen of petrol settles here ever so gentle.

O gently now still float the fumes over the public trees
and the public seats therefore

it is an open stillness right down here under the girdered
grip of the sky where cold edges of buildings and motors

flail by

on the other (wild) side of that band of leafy trees
still feeding off them metallic bees

that are getting nowhere   fast.

Auto/fellatio flippancies of 'the good guys'
running rings round Auckland you vast arse
                                                    / *soul*

you've got your very own marketable twist
here at the top O' the Isle,

never a truer phrase passed than the HAURAKI Gulf:

you know,
someone oughta build a Radio Station Heir   *(ha ha)*.

•• ••

They've slapped a contraceptive writ on Aotea Clinic
while a darkening flood of women drag ripe bellies off

the international tarmac and down the long slide
to the Sydney skyscrapers incisive in the surgical light

for there is something in the air over the Tasman
a free/load of immigrants

an airborne web/like gauze of foetal parachutists
raining down, still fallen on another soil.

•• ••

When the city has become one fluorescent tube
the Black Concentrations blockade the Gulf.

Islands and islands coast out of the bluestone waters
which slide like an abacus the tides,

the tides that short/change with spillage of distance
the numerous beaches here.

Rangitoto has a secret stash of water which no living soul
has seen or smelt, perhaps fed by the dark stream

that ran the course of Queen Street when Auckland
was nothing but scrub and Ti tree,

when Auckland was nothing. Now, in a thousand basements
buildings pump back the unseen sea unseen, back

to the thrumming tides before folk here get salt
in wounds and nostrils. Auckland is returning to the sea

undercover of dark, undercover of the eternal trig/stations
which mark out the cold boundaries of the sky

and this town won't end with a bang, but smooth as any jingle
open-ended.

7.5 ON THE RICHTER SCALE

A metal/rod the colour of cloud vibrates on the trees.

'Raw ore' is the grain of birdsong fed back to the leaves.

And how the whole construction breaks

and how the entire circuitry runs out upon
the sounding board of air.

Live/wires everywhere and a tonnage of breathing space.
From the harbour, ships sound out horns and depart

against the mist and along the metal/rod of cloud.

Through the Black Concentrations of Auckland
the metal/rod the colour of cloud vibrates like a tuning fork.

Tuneless,
the sounds gather into flatness and the whole construction
breaks.

MOSAIC

The colour plate of Auckland pressed against that cupola.

On the air and in that vibration
how the line distorts—

the inverted images of the city dropped into the round.

And how the enamel cubes express their light
within the dark fan of the sky, and how!

There ain't nothing antique about this city when it has become

                    one fluorescent tube

even in reflection is sliding back to the sea
into prebiotic ruin.

O to slip quietly from the face of the sky and break the surface

and break the waters

and break the capillary tubes of the nostrils of the people here.

O to break recognition with one another (like a memory restored).

PERSPECTIVE

The physicist will tell you:
                    God is matter of fact
equals
          /
          no one need be surprised at guilt anymore, quoth
the lay poet.

The explanation holds the centre together.

Surprise: fear: suicide: surprise.
And that's an equation like the man

arms and legs in salute of the air over and over the same problem
and so I remind myself that I must remind myself

   • the astronaut yawns life onto the universe

   • the poet draws breath back out of the earth

   • the sail surfer plays the division between earth and sky.

ASCENSION

Rangitoto does not possess light.

Rangitoto (sparkles as a tube of crystal water) inside.

Rangitoto absorbs itself.

•• ••

The baked charcoal island weighted on the bluestone harbour
brittle as the fluorescent tube

as the gulls lift over to it that something in the air.

Rangitoto of The Dead Ones / the seventh seal of the barren uteri
you would expect to explode colour like a Japanese graphic.

'A great mountain, all in flame'.

THE FIND

for Hone Tuwhare

They dug her up in Queen Street.
A fossilised colonial woman clutching a parasol,
stiff and rigid in her flannel frock.

Pince-nez clay encrusted on the bridge
of her nose, she was pointed toward
Alexandra Park, English settler fashion

when the pneumatic bursts shattered the
ear bone. A couple of spades and they wedged
her out of the mould (intact)

and leaned her against the side of a
Kenworth and then broke for smoko—
propped there as though to advertise it.

She was carbon dated 1863, and by the salt stains
on her handkerchief (tucked under the sleeve)
she had either been crying or spending

too much time with the boys down at the
Whaling Station. Records failed to prove this.
One thing remained a mystery to authorities:

the stake, or rather, surveyor's peg
driven through the breast bone, attested
to an acquisitive quarrel over which

were her rights, and which weren't?

EARTHBOUND MIRRORS

[i]

In these days, we don't exult the sun.

Instead, we pay cheap coinage to
its reflection and I'm reminded

that there ain't nothing new on a metaphor.

Who would dare praise the sun
that something close to our hearts?

Exult him then!

That great runner who sees the track before him
and that makes me feel real proudful.

In these days, we don't exult the sun.

A man shot in the snow will distort
like a hall of mirrors   I mean;

there's just too much other beauty about.

[ii]

A woman polished as an earthenware jug
filled with northern light:

and you know   there isn't a chance of that.
Is that what beauty's all about

what you'd like to give into most
to make a gift of it, to get what's going?

Right through your eyes   allow me
to see these transparencies

which crush me like ice. *Now, that's beauty.*

And so I practise at departure
as this light moving the trees—airily.

What saves me (if you can call it that)
are the words here which stick,

something like a rubber/boot on damp ash.

[iii]

O the renown of the writer who put it:
'the arse end of nowhere'

this place which has light through
it as the wet across the back of a fish

and the whole damn island   rising.

The arse end of nowhere has got this
geological radiance, the likes of which

make an unwritable thesis.
The sun is resin all over the day it bubbles

and all over these pencil/scrapings
which have the sound of laughter.

O the renown of the chorus who sang it.

[v]

I turn my back on the world
my tendons between the shoulder/blades

set me against the poking of this planet

like any other. I am a small corner into
which the noises of the continents

gather and eddy.
I turn my back on the world and feel

the sharp blows on the back of the neck,
in this way, I add to the noises of the earth.

I drive my centre to the eye of your hurricane.

(I say) that our love is a little
like a summit meeting, we swap histories,

we bargain for terms. Our own separate
bag of noises we throw at each other as

so many sticks and stones to break our bones
and with sudden percussion fall upon one another.

[vii]

Our bodies move through one single arc of sorrow.
(Forgive) them who haven't noticed a whit.
                                    /
                              Brother!
Now that's about as meek and mild as you can get:

like people setting up road blocks

like fright stretched to a piano wire

like people holding out against themselves

and I won't let go of you till you let go of me
yes I will no I won't yes I will you to the devil.

Our bodies move through one single arc of regret,
c'mon   be fair   that's only afterwards.

Sister, I tell you that for the moment
them bells toll to kick the shit out of us (gently).

[xi]

Here I am then,
a spotted handkerchief and stick on my shoulder

the southern/hemisphere like a cairn behind me.

I whistle a merry tune
into the corners of the world sniff the prospects

my heart the colour of camouflage.
Under indifferent stars I don a different hat

buried as a worm in the northern half of this apple
I digest another set of sins.

Here I am then,
a spotted handkerchief and stick on my shoulder

O ever so slightly worse for wear.

BLACK CONCENTRATIONS

Morning, noon, evening who drinks the milk of darkness?

I consider the magic or aggression
gone out of it—entirely. Lives, that is.

A distinct peace.

The immediate slowed to peace / sans / colour.

Stillness plump as a cushion not sat upon.

Understanding if you wish and that is what you wish.

So much habitation and no one to hear me observe
and no one to inform me they do not hear me say

what sort of peace is this?

I am a small area of agitation. I am here
and everyone finding nourishment in other places.

Evening, noon, and morning who drinks the milk of darkness?

Vienna, 1979

SANG THE SAIL SURFER

Wherein that zone of coming toward
(not quite rainbow) where all is possible

possession takes place the colours running
and the boundaries non-existent

and at once the reach of prophecies is present
before final settled things begin before

corybantic moon and the sun remunerative
resume their different and separate reserves.

And only then is the air tight with warning.

No hour can be appointed to this time
which decides against the rhythms of day

as the mind reels out in perfect balance
and with itself (is sought out in turn)

and at once the reach of prophecies is present
a woman will foretell who plays with light

this is the song of the Black Concentrations
in the scooped hollow at the back of the head.

And only then is the air tight with warning.

GUARDIANS, NOT ANGELS

WALTZING THE GODS

As if they could not lift themselves high enough
children who unfold into fantasies

kites over Philopappou Hill
from string, pull cloud out of thin air

the way a comma tugs when the line runs out.

The clouds I spoke of, augmented, became italic
and passed through the stilled serif of the Acropolis

as did the kites that worked the air—*bluish*
like the freshly exposed socket of a bone.

As if they could not lift themselves high enough
where sideways

a 747 snipped to view and halved the sky
and cut the string that played the fingers that lifted

the hands that tossed the kites the children built.

Behind certain white walls you can hear
the untroubled plumbing of the flute

and you would propose that here, the player
transposed fingertips to a flock of doves.

Or at certain quaysides,
brake drums within the throats of mules, screech.

On the sounding board of these cobbled ways (that is)
from the whitewashed alleyways

noisy with the approach of mules, events of sound.

Then the heavy swallowing of the bell tower
makes solid the hour and you would conclude that

it was here events had collected
as though people, objects exchanged substances.

As marble broke down against the skyline,
broken and suggestive of an absent architecture

the half dome of the observatory rose—frozen,
locked up the moon for the night on an empty sky.

And the Acropolis, silent as a construction site,
held down the curled blueprint of the stars

a tiny model made to house a universe while
over Philopappou Hill closed the dark shutters of bats:

closed the theory of darkness we call night

opened the small recognitions we call the stars

parted the vast separations we call the winds

revolved the minute gravities we call stillness.

Ano Petralona, Athens 1979

ACE

Sky ploughs and grades to
partial storm, quick moments
of darkness, casual rain.
An aircraft drags badly taped
sound through another hour.
The engine rocks its mounts
confident. The prop turns,
autodidactic. Quartz landing
lights calculate a downward
path. An early idiom of
stars surface upward. He gives
his scarf one comic flick,
college style. He taxis in.
By planets and galaxies of gas-
light he dreams ambition
high as a stealth bomber,
swerves o'er massy thunderhead.
With eyes blitzed as Beirut
his gatling laughter strafes.
Or, tearing a dotted line
down the Dead Sea—noise
chasing after—he sways that
horizon cradle fashion, sweeps
the Left Bank, banks to the
Apollo glare of the Sinai high
noon. He dreams his family
safely bunkered and quartered
suburb wise, happy as a neatly
clipped hedge, kids hopping
Frisbee quick on the broad lawn.
His spouse, blond as bread,
awaits the whisperings of his
black box heart, mooning for
dog fight love at home coming.

A FAR NOISE FROM NEAR THINGS

That which has gained a little
further, high enough to curve out the
earth, the diminished rainforests

of Brazil, the hole in the ozone above
Antarctica, the lessened bush tribes of
Africa, the years pushed out by light,

the greenhouse globe over-photographed
is how we picture ourselves back,
falling. Or rice paper moon in the

July afternoon. Bulkheads of tankers
white lit on the horizon. Night,
underground with a silence of escalators.

Sky and cloud, a dream of snakes.
A fallen leaf against the skylight.
A leaf against the skylight fallen, so.

And we then who engage the light
take ourselves to the work of aerial
attention the Ancients were part of—

remembrance of time, atomistic.
The seasons knew us as we learned.
Our lessons learned well, too.

Around the roulette wheel of the world,
through the yellow pages of the sun flicking
over decades what migrations made,

from the microchip to Star Wars,
digital sex to right wing abstinence;
eclipse of personal vision, limitation of

immediate memory, the object of
our desires objective love, love at several
removes in our falling. *Sangsara.*

The great lesson came in a sudden hurt
of killing, our first knowledge
reflected through caves ochre images

of the slain. We began worship,
measured time, and built against the
shock, the pain. These sentiments amongst

the tumbled blocks of older verse are
gone from the heart, the darkest galaxy,
and memory alone promotes sorrow.

It is today always, green as a computer
screen and elsewhere, unrecorded,
the high surgery of the supernova which

never exploded now, but once.
Child dream. An abandoned railway
siding overgrown with nettle, hide-

out for a wizard. Backdrop of gentle
slopes, elms at distance.
Adolescent visions of Irish barrows,

hollowed darkness, whisperings, a wish
to locate the signal in self back in time.
This resides still. Downwards and over

the garden (a dark, humped square)
my neighbour shadows through drop blinds
before a startled TV. Dirtied cloud

frames a full moon that is sideways in
this movingly. Gravity takes hold
and accentuates. Gestures weigh in their

orbits. Bright as cufflinks, radio
telescopes revolve on red tablelands
to uncover one more sacred site between

the stars. A brain-based society
ornately tracks the lusty technologies
and the years recognise our whereabouts.

In the beginning wooden paddles echoed
from atoll to island. Air whitened,
thunder reverberated. A riot of leaves

under malarial rain. Then came the
creak of rigging, came the offshore
companies, came synthetic drugs

and salvation, and finally, came migration
back to Vanuatu, Samoa, Tonga, Niue
to light up the rim of the Pacific.

The hour turns, an electric train flicks
blue flashes over suburb and hoarding,
brick arch and emptied streets.

The day's news ceases amongst the
satellites. High enough to curve out earth,
painted prows of long boats are falling

on southern skies, dragging their keels
across some coral harbour where—fitfully,
gracious guns of goodwill ride at anchor.

Chelmsford Street, Newtown, Sydney, 1987

Behind some night bush Rousseau green,
some dwelling in one place, some in another,
it had been agreed between us by courier
and hesitation to meet in the village centre
at midnight. The first figure to emerge
was to be greeted thus: *America comes to
interpret its humour*: the hurried reply;
community halls abound. Back, beyond our
allotted frequency, the general who had
not been posted gathered over another power
lunch. After the brief and the oiling of
rifles we set forth across the causeway
through the marble green of foothills,
into the grey of higher ground. The thought,
like a saffron scarf caught on a thorn
bush seemed even now on the closed terrain a
crusade of sorts—kept us ahead. Amply,
unnumbered rivers plashed into the battery
green of immeasurable hollows. So it was
that we became inseparable, spirit creatures
to the forest life, the journey boundless,
the orders which concerned the depot, unread.

HALLO MOON, *HALLO MOON*

Janis Joplin had duende, made her feel
good but can you take it? The Stone Age people
worshipped the heart, hard line love of elements.

The vision meets the image perfectly.
MOON BOUNCING radio operators call it—Kepler
dreamed this too. Signals bounce back visually.

If you've the right equipment you become
the man without qualities, a prism in your hand.
You don't know the weight of heartwood.
And, who do you love anyway? You went past
your original, became mud only to become human
once more. Something remembered you.
With a kind of irradiance, your soft focus
fell back upon me through an arch of greenery.

NICHOLAS CHARLES BOCHSA 1789-1856

Camperdown Cemetery, Sydney

I liked your story and the
stone placed by your lover, Ann
Bishop, in St Stephen's cemetery.
How Ann left her composer
husband Henry to his knighthood
and in Paris found you, Nicholas
Bochsa. You became lovers,
travelled the continent giving
concerts, she with her magical voice
and you with your lyre. Then you
sailed on to Sydney and your final
curtain call at the *Royal*.
Did the 'Agents of Napoleon' truly
track you down under, pay you
off for crimes of embezzlement?
You knew return to France meant
immediate arrest and jail.
Knowing you were dying you wrote
your own requiem, a loud laugh
at Catholicism. After, Ann gave you
an Anglican burial and the whole
town turned out. She never looked
back, continued on to China.
So you took thousands from the
emperor, shows you knew a good rort,
were pretty good with your hands.

Something has lit up your
Motherland. Whose eyes? What flock
of birds? *Camplights?*
Late summer eve and the freeway
insists its traffic through wind.
Rubbed off sound. Handfuls of
enjoyment coming and going.
Not the noise of barbed wire dragged
through snow, and not the dull
weight of concrete at Zone 4 Mordovia.
Irina Ratushinskaya, would this
have reached your last address
before your Russian God brought you
safe to England, and safely to
her hospitals, to the *free world* and a
million little decisions?
Handfuls of shouting reach out from
solitary confinement, your breath
amplifies and your words
bite warmth. Something has lit up
your Motherland.

AND ALL THE GOODTIME CHARLIES

for my mother, Cecily Joan McCormack, 1921-1990

Striding girls spill from
office blocks, cool light through
May leaves. The moon, a hayrick
unsettled before palings of cloud.
A bat caught on wire makes
one buckled lampshade.
Your generation ends with you now.
Swell, so long! I see chrome hubs
spinning backward along green
embankments under a tribute of elm.
Something carries through laughter
like a klaxon, and shuffles
black swans over the Taieri River.
The town clock ceased sometime
back in 1920, when brassy sounding
trams halted by the Band Rotunda.

THE DECADEERS

Yi-yippee-yo! The picket line of
verse slingers stretches back to the '50s.
The decadeers ride on in anthological
gallop to blaze the way with found
poetry into one more famous sunset.
Kerouac is laid back on the trail, strung
out beneath the Bo Tree. Bukowski has
lit out for the Badlands of LA.
Stead's skull hangs over the ripped off
limbs of embryo poets at El Academia.
Jacques Derrida signs up, notches
a trope on the butt of language—
they ride on off the page onto the stage.
All that day smoke rose untroubled
from the desk top mesas into a blank sky.
In the borderless regions the racist
ape yawled through the stadiums of Europe.
Then night came fast as a fax,
and as they leaned into saddles on that
wordless waste, each writer pondered: what
had been altered by the observation of it?
The *furor poeticus* sang like a
great wind down the Information Highway.

ISLANDS OF WILDERNESS—A ROMANCE

15.   *Grafton, Auckland, 1981*

Love is a way back
to the first sense before
association, beyond the large,
lit city of mind, to
departure before it became
loss, to memory before it became
sorrow, and so on back to
original models before we bought
the bright, imitative ones.
On hearing the above,
her brow arched into a bow,
dismissively. His discoveries
sank, this in turn gave
rise to pity, and so on.

29.

Then the rats up and left.
Much later, the Pied Piper
and the townsfolk,
following upon the greedy heels
of illusion, walked into
the mountain. Tough.
So she plays the song she wants
to hear inside another's head.
Or did. Until the echo
came back like a boulder telling
the same old story:
in the beginning was The Word
for those with heart enough
to hear.

32.

DEAR LADY, regard my heart
as a waiting room. The
magazines lie fanwise on
the empty seat. The poster
reads: SAVE THE BEECH FORESTS.
An undergrowth of light through
bamboo blinds warms
the body's mind. My hands
make an appointment with your
breasts, and that mountainous
plateau of exquisite flowers
where you hail me from.

35.

All the tough kids got
married and made a homework
full of kids who went to school
and got tough and didn't
believe what mum and dad said.
I let loose my dart at you.
But the message inside was too
heavy and I missed. I wanted
to say I would walk you
home because that's where
the heart is, and, if I am
to find yours—it's the first
place I would look.

44.

In the ancient city of Jaffa
yellow steps descend to the whale's
belly, to white weddings in cool,
stone rooms. *Shalom*. Between
the explosions and the weather
life is matter-of-fact. But today
space is tense and boasts occupation,
like bunkers built on the moon.
At the dead centre of this
amphitheatre the echo laps back
from my feet.
            Unavoidable.

47.

Under the mineral waters
of the moon, valid is the ordinary
vision, and the vision ordinaire
over the clean night. What shall
we allow? Now I've got you
telescoped I recognise my wants,
and the fear that all is possible.
No truths here babe, only
contrasts. I guess that, now the
contract is out, I need a certain
grace to finish the job?

58.*

On her sad
pilgrimage she leans into
hills on her way home, forever
bent against nostalgia, to
where she has always been, that
childhood round as a world.
Impossible now. And this is why
she is still going,
caught there on the track
under the green cliff, as
though it were merely a day's
walk away.

*Under the original title, Romances, No 58 was taken by
the New Zealand painter, Tony Fomison (1939-1990)
as title and dedication to a work which depicted this scene.*

61.   *Awatea Rd, Parnell, Auckland, 1983*

The Orient (lighted beads
quickly flipped through the hands
of darkness) Express.
The gentleman with the black
fedora didn't move a muscle.
The lady with diamond
fingers, languished. And then, the
thin-lipped man. A hiss
of steam under the vaulted roof.
The dream ended abruptly on
a high note as the lady slumped
forward onto the sign:
R18. SUITABLE FOR ADULTS ONLY.

A Night of Warehouses.
The wind of God blows through
ventilation ducts rank as
carbolic. Lucky Luciano makes
a deal with Dutch Schultz.
Rat-ta-tat-tat-tat.
'Even if you ain't seen it,
you've heard it all before.'
'Sure, it reminds me of
a dream I never had.'
And the two old priests drink
and roll dice and each harbours
a gangster in his heart.

78.

On the dark side of a
cold hill *(they sang)* bullets
were the one light, and roses
blossomed from out his chest
(they sang) against a green,
green sky. He dreamed then
of being tossed into the Spanish
night on the horns of the sun.
Federico Garcia Lorca,
the most humble of village fountains
lifts its sword to clash
against the icicles of the moon,
your silence.

86.   *Chelmsford St, Newtown, Sydney, 1988*

Rain solid as riot gear
on beach palms, the day flexible
under Cyclone Gaddafi.
A landing barge pulls to the cove
and the General proclaims
a Banana Republic.
Props: pink canvas chairs and
lettuce green towels.
Back on Lava Mountain natives
fire up the Bicentennial Beacon.
The South Pacific sure has
a lot to answer for but—
that's cool.

87.

'Look pal, men do it
for prestige, and women for
security, so write that across
the sky. Both demand different
things, relationships, that is.'
  —*Le Roman de la Rose*—
was rooted out centuries ago, killed
off with a high powered mix
of cynicism and freedom.
In fact, the last couple seen
heading into the labyrinth
was Laurel and Hardy,
looking terribly confused.

91.

Tank tracks down the
arm of Afghanistan. Supertankers
plunge into the Persian Gulf.
We forever enact a terrible
knowledge, that all of us contain
the negative of the Big Bang,
are those self-same atoms.
Energy continuously surfaces as
anger, creation turned inside-out.
Sacred domes on the
highest mountains revolve toward
that farthest point of
fleecy light.

94.

Disappointment hung
slack like rope on a bollard.
Town Planners downed pens
when we missed out on the America's
Cup. Seminal designs for the
Auckland harbour boulevard
went up in smoke.
And when *Mlle Leprieur* blew up
the Rainbow Warrior she got
the gitaway holiday to a
South Pacific Hideaway.
Now she's home & pregnant, a
little live corpse afloat
inside her.

98.

Sails whiter than an
Opera House tilt toward the
continent flat as a postage stamp,
lift to the Centre Point Tower.
Discovery Day is, what it is.
And give the blacks the old heave-ho
in the wake of the first fleet.
There's the balloon hike
and Expo 88, there's the woodchip
graft from a grateful parliament,
futons and Snugglepot Awards.
Discovery Day is, what it is.
And give the blacks the old heave-ho
in the wake of the first fleet.

UNMANNED

GENERATION OF '68

Frank O'Hara (here I'm skating slow
on sacred ice) has got a lot to answer
for, yet who hasn't? Take the legacy
of '60s poets, for example, who can't
help but write like him; syntactically
careering around his blizzard of words,
elbow jolting crazily, clutching at
each other's ear muffs, buttonholing
opportunity. Seems they did that as
par for the course till it got too dizzy.
Round and round the freedom rink they
went, those who zigzagged quick, cut
up rough, fell back upon the railings
youth exhausted to exhale worn, cautious
success though tried not to show it.
What happened to the stragglers in the
maul is anyone's guess; some unmarried,
a good number courted hardship. Whatever.
Nobody cares overly much. The '60s poets,
they go on to write like Frank 0'Hara:
fewer drop by parties, meaner somehow.

PAT BOONE & TONTO

White shirted (not blue)
they approach in twos:
'Excuse me sir, a small
moment of your time?'
Soft selling eternity &
the clean-cut Hereafter.
The boyish accent downloads
the serious side of the
American dream, eyes fixed
computer bright. The other
is slower, slope shouldered
and discipled, backgrounded
by a blandished brain.
As a child, when the God
was always friendly,
big as a house, long as a
street and the day endless,
the knock upon the door
signalled: 'Excuse me
young man, is the lady of
the house in?' Welcome
the suitcase salesman the
Bon Brush Man: big bristled,
wooden backed scrubbing
and bottle brushes, sandsoap
and Brasso for hard domestic
usage. Not now. These two
modern pedlars head out
to the brick bungalows of
the inner city suburbs
selling the Light and the Way,
galloping round the outer
handicapped districts;
brainwashed right wing angels
confident as professional
sportsmen on a World Tour.

WORDS TO LURE A GHOST

Henley Pub? I am one year from
your death, and a mad mile from your
achievement
                    twenty or so years
down the track. I think you may have
killed a few of us off, brother,
who rejoiced
in your thicket of sorrows.
                              Jim Baxter,
if a cabbage tree marks your spot by
the river,
                    I am glad of it.
After you went, we were too eager
for another Apollo, and the laurel
was tossed from
hand to poetic hand like a hot kumara.
Most dropped it. A number were swept
by the winter river with the eels
into the Underworld.
                         The God Love
and the God Vengeance sat down
in a burnt out warehouse to share out the
small morsels
                    of pain.
The poets
                 are playing hide-and-seek
with each other in and out of marriage.
The sharing
                 is done.
                         A southerly
whistles up over the gun emplacements on
Brooklyn Hills,
                 Jim, scattering
the unposted, autumn leaves.

MYTH & MARIOLATRY

At a small village not
far from Manila, in the house
of armaments and munitions,
in a house of grenades
and ammunition, the plaster
statue of the Virgin Mary as
humble as a trademark,
stands splashed in carmine
tears like some peasant
shot on a quiet morning bearing
water from the creek.
The hovels strewn about
the hills are so many broken
boxes. The sun is spinning
clockwise for hope. One
cloud out of nowhere then a
drape of blue that might
be the sky. The gathering of
people is more impressive
than a food drop. They come
at the appointed hour when
the boy who serves as
runner to the Beautiful Lady
arrives, breathless, with
the Word. Occasionally,
the statue weeps paint fresh
tears. They will leave
once faith is gathered in
abundance like so many wild
flowers off the nearest mountain
slope. Here under a glass
blown moon, a cool wind shall
leave this place sacred.

BRAIDWOOD

for Judith Wright

Granite and quartz country, once
gold rush, now cattle tread amongst

the white hawthorn and yellow broom;
from Captains Flat to Majors Creek

the creek beds cut the empty vein.

Hail or heat, the hanged ghost
of Thomas Braidwood rolls out his

oaths big as boulders upon the town:
'dust, poverty, despair, drunkenness'

before he choked his rage at the
end of a rope, phlegm thick as gossip.

WARDROBE DRINKERS

is what they are in Austinmer.
Yuppies from the North Shore $300,000
homes on the beach front sending
the RSL broke and the greenies
blocking development for a few birds
up an estuary. Could be worse,
given the Japs on the Gold Coast
going off like mobile phones.
The miners and cottages—long gone,
so is full employment. In 1941
as a telegraph delivery boy I made
13 shillings 10 a week. Across
the harbour bridge to the North Shore
on a regulation red bike. Sunday
was the day for casualty messages,
the dead and wounded delivered
all over Sydney except Vine Street,
Darlington, where *Darcy the Crim* lived
and the most dangerous place in town.
I came to Austinmer 30 years ago
before the wardrobe drinkers
in the days of the miners and cottages.
Take those grain and coal carriers
upwards of 250,000 tonnes with a 12
man crew, anchored stern to wind,
off Hill 60 out of Port Kembla
navigated by satellite direct to Japan.
You want the best view? Sublime Point
Lookout, right down the coast, the
Pacific ironed flat far as the eye can
see, a sky expanded metal red nightly.

Austinmer, NSW, 1993

AUNTY EV

who always kept the aspidistras
flying high up in her Georgian house on
the windy Terrace from marble urns

          had lipstick bomber pilot red
and nails the colour of flame.

It was often 'elevenses' in her lounge
with Gordon's served on a silver platter,
THE CITY HOTEL, DUNEDIN 1932 engraved

on the rim. 'Another "stim" dear?'
from the mahogany sideboard repository to dozens
of weighty 78 jazz records in brown paper
jackets stacked like so many ossified flapjacks.

Oh she had the most beautiful hands (in her day)
they said, used for commercials in the
Woman's Weekly and Boots the Chemists.

Who could forget her gravel voice and make up
mannequin thick—

        not remember her gin sweet
breath warm upon the neck? And how some yank
billeted during WWII (here) 'ducky!'
thought she was a 'real living doll'.

Such beautiful hands she had and the crystal light
streaming forth from those great bay windows

onto the iron railings below.

Great to have met Joseph Conrad
or for that matter, H.G. Wells, who said,
*'Let's go upstairs and do nice things
with our bodies,'* and who did just
that to take a tilt at the waitress.
I saw them once, Conrad & Wells, in
a photograph, standing together.
A courtyard setting beside a few bamboo
chairs. The hour was mild in a black
and white afternoon. Trees, too,
green galleons shipping oars in autumn.
Conrad had, perhaps, cast off the last line
of a novel: the indigo lump upon the
horizon is an island: behind it the sun
spilling its treasure trove: the rent
sailcloth of a sea squall. Anyway,
he could still smell the coast wobble from
the deck of the tartane, her weight
to the wind. Wells, maybe, was thinking on
socialism and science, and in some
melancholic way of the waitress, her
scent. By what conversations did
they measure each other, these two voyagers
who possessed that sense of the bigness
of the world? For Wells, an electrical
spark that arced across the white page,
for Conrad, each word creaking on
the blocks, the woman pale before the moon,
her eyes black as tornadoes at sea.

least, that's what the Old Londoner
told me who didn't learn to relax till well
past fifty, seated alongside his two
mates: a Norwegian: 'You're not the same
person now as you were ten years ago.'
And the Irishman: 'I like the music it's
the noise I can't stand.' Each one,
orphaned, aphoristic, deep into his sixties.
NZ born and much younger, I offered:
'You're not the same person tomorrow as
you were today.' And then, 'To your
arrival in Melbourne,' they singly toasted.
(Great grandfather, McCormack, arrived
here in 1851 and 26 years later, in 1877, set
sail for Dunedin aboard the *Ringarooma*).
So our tale of the two cities unfolded:
Sydney is get what you can. Melbourne,
what have you got to offer and are we really
interested. The afternoon floated by
as did the trams with dry, asthmatic rush
in this mellow town of bungalows and brass.

Melbourne, 1993

BRUNO LAWRENCE

Bruno, do you remember the *Me and Gus* stories,
way before Barry Crump got keen, when a cow cocky
was a bastard you met on gravelly roads? Recall
the nights playing community halls, and days making
a few records, only to break a few more? 'Ricky
May's Jazz Combo', 'Max Merritt & The Meteors',

'Quincy Conserve', plus, the all-stars-road-show
Blerta† travelling Aotearoa, through khaki paddocks,
down thistle blown highways in that diesel bus.
Seasonal rhythms you doubtless gathered, drummer
extraordinaire, on your final journeying off Cape
Reinga, the spirit freed to ride the rain—you backed

the loner to the last, death the bottom line to stave
off cancer. *Bruno, you did that thing*. R&B, jazzman,
film star (didn't Jack Nicholson say get on over
to Hollywood?) but you preferred back-blocks, sought
small towns, river shingle, the hollows of the land,
and a home around Waimārama in the Hawkes Bay.

A shifting romantic, hoon and hangman, real joker,
you played yourself sans bullshit in a heap of movies;
'Wild Man,' where you leapt from life to art
without a hitch; 'Smash Palace', 'The Quiet Earth',
how you loved women, warmth by the bus load,
and covered that classic—*my 10 inch, record of the blues.*

† *Bruno Lawrence's Electric Revelation and Travelling Apparition.*

THE STILL WATCHES

III

Who can offer words unsullied
by the age like the sad integrity of
a Graham Greene? Generations
pass on into uncharted waters, the
lights out along the deck.
Behind, the floodlit logging of
Malaysia gluts the Japanese market.
Ahead, seals choke in the heavy metal
swell of the Baltic Sea;
or through a destiny as choppy as a
Berryman sonnet, the earth
seemed unearthly in a hold of love lashed to
the bulkheads of youth one time,
O it was some time ago. But now,
the hour hangs out centre stage, a
cat whiskered moon doffs into
darkness and ushers in a Qantas jumbo
to Kingsford Airport, down the runway
to Eastern Standard Time, and a
continent the memory of elsewhere.

Welcome tourists to the whirl
of Kings Cross, a caged fan spinning
the night through, shredding the
Sydney dreamers. Out along THE WALL
you can solicit your nightlong
visas where the bare-chested boys
thrust hips from the bonnets
of old Holdens. High up on the
bulging stonework and boldly sprayed:
'It's going to rain tonight, so
take a bullet proof vest,' or,
'No war on the way, only a change in

76

the weather.' Welcome the
eagle-eyed predators come to roost
in the coops of the cities.
Let us go down to the docks again to
the fat silos that overshadow
Iron Cove Bridge, toward the Inner
Harbour, where craft coloured
and alive on the paint box waterways
streak around and about, caught
up against the shark net constructions
of Patrick White. Welcome the waves
of early morning fog that break
upon the sky gardens, and the ironclad
poppy of Centre Point Tower.

VI

He will come urgent as a food
riot. Beware the man who sheds tears of
mercury. His cough alone will thin
out the ozone. He grips oceans with
the black fingers of trawlers.
His voice is a slow leakage in the Third
World night. Beware the waste broker.
He comes to paint your wellsprings
ivory black and chrome yellow. You will
know him by his industrial oath:
'$40 a drum! yes, only $40 a drum!'
Senegal, Nigeria, West Africa,
the sun dangerous as a 40 gallon drum.
Drums stacked on rotting pallets
in the back yard of tropical forests.
Drums swollen like the bellies
of starved children with toxic waste.
Under the red copper basin of the sun,
under the broken crockery of stars,
Senegal, Nigeria, West Africa.

Meanwhile, George MacDonald flees
the evil wood through the unreflecting
mirror of 19th century time, a
prophet of the cinema. O cine romance!
Tony Curtis (sword glint of light
off teeth) and Natalie Wood, beautiful
in white tulle (lungs not yet waterlogged)
in heady love. Follow their laughter
with an open-top Lagonda down
the white walled roads of Mount Etna to
the Port of Catania—a blood boiling
swerve to the red chequered table,
fishing boats moored in the blue dusk.
Woody Allen steps from the screen
to the dead crystal lakes of Sweden. A
wavering moon disc lies reflectèd
there under an Excalibur beam of light.
Clouds, too. Those ancient purities
across my triptych window-view-of-the-sky
package air as light as Styrofoam.
The lighthouse beam chills the sand hills
and oceans gather up whale breath
to cloud. Our civilisation bartered on
the whale's back. Love undrinkable as water.
The silent film of fantasy which is night
plays out through the ivory keys of stars.

IX

Sun shines metallic off Footscray
and out across West Gate Bridge. Silver
and green office blocks rise from a
dun plain. Superman, bearing a stash of
old money darts over the dockside
and the hidden sea home to Melbourne.
The thought of you adds weight
to new memory—sad as lamplight on rain

sodden guttering. Sadder still is the
romantic soul lapsed to obscenity,
the swine tides that clog the spirit.
Again, I drive my centre to the eye
of your hurricane. Remember how
the senses wrangled, anger like a vicious
exorcism of betrayals not worded?
To run is to hide is to freely admit the
hidden hurt. Volscian woman, we flung our
fire at each other heavy as fists.
The old man sits in the park feeding
pigeons; like his memories, they are
grey blue and flutter about him.
My memory of you from any perspective
falls along the flat face of this earth.
No lamp lit up our consciousness,
only the blade figured the light, Psyche.

'The funeral of the sea'
sings the Italian documentary. The
world's rotting oil fleet blanks
out the Mediterranean from the French
coast to the Bay of Naples. Six
hundred burning black candles turn crude
the Arab night and Red Adair pots
another well. Oil Magnates!
Corporate Cowboys! Have you built your
little ship of death, O have you?
There in the deep the great underwater
colonialist, Jacques Cousteau, laments
the dark night of the sea, his
eyes are the colour of basalt.
Today we have part-time cloud and the
hours work at it cruel as barbed wire drawn
across the face of the moon.
What then is this other? It is
the shadow personality, 'evil comes from

the power of evil.' It is the third
presence. O Romance of the World.

XII

O to wish upon a falling space
shuttle! The sky tries hard to reveal
itself as bluestone, but temperature
and wrappings of cloud are against it.
Rain falls hard as luck. Here you will
see them lift up, a squadron of
pigeons swinging to gun the light, wings
ablaze, the bulky horizon thunderous
where thunder lies cognisant.
The Great Dividing Range runs this way
and I am on the lee side toward the
sea. The setting sun awakens our
ancestral demand for bonfires
big as cities, and a leisurely parade
of gulls passing overhead mistake
the darkening hours for sea cliffs.
These coastal towns boast the best burgers,
the newest surf club—while the RSL
bends to the heavy metal swell which
runs the raft of every sea slap
every weekend. The short, broad streets
are abandoned early to the blue
phosphorescence of the TV and the evening
rustle of newspapers. Tomorrow,
of course, is uninhabited and fresh as a
child's drawing. Further on through
the minutes someone is hard at a hammer as
if wanting to be let in. A news
bulletin tells of avenues long as decades
in a steepled town where tanks gather,
ready to break through a hay barn

in Kosovo. (Remember the Revolutionary
Poet * who broke through a crowd?)
No, this is only a rusted keel upended
in the quarter acre backyard. Not
by some turbulence round Cape Horn but
the tedium of a bankrupt dream loose as a
cloud. The family seams have now sprung
apart and the kids school the public
bars. A day in the round for the father who
breaks through the top-shelf like a
picket line. At the local cinema watch the
astronaut yawn, unaware the alien
prepares to storm the spaceport wordless as
a threat. It's dusk here, mist drowns
streetlights, the earth for a time puts aside
its hunger, and a delayed flight
fills in for the evening star of autumn.

Vladimir Mayakovsky

NEW POEMS: 1998–2000

OLDEST PINE

*A 10,500-year-old Huon pine, believed to be the world's oldest
tree, was handed back to Tasmania yesterday by mining
company Pasminco.*
—Sydney Morning Herald, April 24, 1998

Years grew in rings,
but my earliest memories
sought bird dialect, the
hush of water and wind.

Men could hear then,
stood with forest silence;
the leaf-like breathing
at my base made speech.

The loud and glacial
grumbling of boulder—
ice ceased in my first years,
ferns eventually uncoiled.

I thought myself *ever*
which is now at a closing;
yet I did not regard
this end without mystery.

Other pine trees that
built memory in fire onto
their bark's surface,
recorded an earlier time;

they hide mostly in the
moist gullies and deep rift
valleys (branches radial):
an ancient pine tree.

Unchanged—whose
photo is found locked in
the earth's element, an old
family and they are few.

The wide branched
rivers that angled mirrors
under the sun, are gone
underground, they

emerged from within
the ice tides, mountains fell
when the sky opened, the
seas had retreated.

They are shadow leaves.
They flow many branched.
They house every myth.
They rise in me to air.

THIS WAY

That nightly sound is something
else, hardly a series of chords, though
through waves slur into a particular
noise as through a lopsided mouth;

motor bike, bus, laughter or scream.
Yet underpinning this, that same uniform
growl going nowhere intentionally
but into itself, back into the city.

If you could see them, you'd know
that those boot scuffed clouds are the
dirty bits left over from the day;
a star holds to the sky's rounded toe,

more stars and it's steel capped.
It took centuries for the cities to get to
this, from easy camp fire cluster,
shield and spear clatter or wood crackle.

Once the guttural rasps of *yes*
and *no* had coagulated into walled images,
the blaze of blood and light gave over
to these arteries, to the vessels of glass.

The old migratory paths are soon
rediscovered by armies in triumphal
procession through the broad thoroughfares,
and under arches as though into caves.

'This way,' it says, 'this way,'
a call that is at once all utterance or
none, a deep cave sound, the primal rumour,
conspiracy, beginnings, heat and cold.

85

COPESTONE FOR A NATION

Here is the place which flourished once in rampant
dishonesties, and there stands the sheared monument
erected to important absences, boldly the canker creeps
and, like the last of the sun's rays, heat fabricates
a welcoming where none existed before, no traveller

passed by these ruins, no winding silk road or camel
track, no ancient canal, only an endless sheep spill
over river shingle, dogs heard working the memory with
river boulder, that turns deeply, cold and hollowing;
cloch—the same sound found in every river valley.

While the hill terraces make some sort of corbelled
framework for this scene, though slightly faded
below, aslant upon the wall of recollection, behind glass
(the car window) winding down toward what appears
a solitary copse, to an indecipherable, ox-bow signature.

While autumn sets up its garage sale with the season's
odds and ends, gravity leans into distortion; first orange,
then pale yellow, a row of poplars shuffling close
over the lake road, vying for another golden moment in
the aging process, the putty coloured cliffs behind you.

Autumnal orange, yellow, black, as the first primitive
frescoes from the ochre quarries, dank as rust or the
smell of dead oxygen, these poplars lead this valley out
onto the flood plains, birthplace of the city, upon whose
heights the first rituals of praise were offered up as

thanks against the flooding to each and every localised,
individual god or climate, and in whose seasonal favours
the inhabitants trusted, the city and the temple as one,
the temple both defence and memory, commemoration of
the river flow and speech, each flood mythically retold.

Further still though dull days of cloud announce your
arrival: wayfarer, a windblown highway, the lantern
on the hook; as now the neon panelled comfort stop fuzzes
with insects, a smell of oil and rubber, no attendant, the
rolled back whites of numerals clicking up the dollars.

Whatever passed this way, has past, passed away in the
direction you're headed, finally—to the cities of the plain;
somewhere, the country breathes largely in the dark
behind the comfort stop. Overhead, the tilting crater lake
of the night sky, stars caught up on its black surface.

EMBLEM FOR DEAD YOUTH

THERE ARE NO EXPERTS ONLY SURVIVORS

Over the past five years in the *Great South Land,*
a primary dissipation of energies; 2,500 youth suicides,
in fact. We pause to consider this phenomenon:

2,500 small white crosses neat as napkins laid
out in geometric patterns upon the parliamentary turf
sweeping up to the *Big House.* Small white crosses,
abstract as wing nuts or butterflies, each one pinned

to the yellow grass lapel though, hauntingly, branded
onto the mind's dumb hide. With each grief prone parent,
pain inflates safe as an air bag. Small towns outback
spin to emptiness. Moonrise is a chalk outline after the

going down of the sun. Stars swing bright herds into the
dark corrals. There's movement at the station; a murmuring
engine through woodland, sky velocity blue as gunmetal.

SALLE D' ATTENTE

a portrait

And what if they didn't meet up,
coupled by the twin lines that seemed
to lead her thoughts endlessly out,
coiling through the Rockies, through

the mountain reaches and conifer;
her lover on the oil rumoured plateau
snowed in, maybe, snowed under
beyond the pass, working his claim?

Luggage stacked on the platform,
hat boxes, portmanteau, steamer trunk
as miniature of her country estate;
she waited the engine's plumed arrival.

Fennel scent stung the nostrils
in the late autumn air, and somewhere,
vaguely distant, a storm detonated
at the peaks, powdered a piece of sky.

No voice reached her through the
October afternoon in that waiting room,
and no one either came or went, only
the signal box mutely shuffled its gears.

THE MANGAWEKAS

After the viaduct was dismantled the
Mangawekas and river valleys stayed on.

The moon maintained its guardianship
under sliding shadow and within the

silent and abandoned hour of night.
That massive boulder set in a creek bed

stands immemorial yet the bevelled
morning light discovers bridge remnants—

an arch truss, a foundation block. You
passed this way before, are not likely to

again. Your footprint on mud dunes
will soften by the next flax woven eddy.

I know of a river bend, and the spread
river shingle slowly flung upon the

slanted afternoon light, handfuls of young
poplars scattered over the valley floor.

On a downward drive through these ranges,
soap grey slate could landslip you off a

hair pin, into this view that the rear vision
mirror spans beneath, or angles before you.

THE GOOD OLD DAYS

The old radiators heat elliptically, green painted
pipes run up the walls with an elbow sleeve right
hand turn (optional) following off where the

ceiling heads, that is, to venetian blinds, eternally
slanting a dirty look at the day and down periscope
through the thick, wide grained floor timbers,

but not before (alongside a wire mesh In/Out tray)
the cardiganed public servant languidly taps his pipe
and pats the tea urn, sips regulation *Dept of*—cups,

while the overhead fan blade stirs and stirs the air:
*Oh, Jane stayed on (marvellous with the Christmas
balloons!) while Dorothy left, a promise of*

*silk stocking and musk. No forwarding, of course,
(except, maybe, the '60s) a leather strapped suitcase
and a railway platform on the overnighter headed*

*God knows where into the interior I shouldn't
wonder (or the suburbs which amounts to the same
thing) to what—tent city? No thoughts on that*

*one Bunty! And no damned prospects most likely,
still she's got her own life to lead.* Those boards now
varnished, the pipes detailed a ruffled and light

grey; swanky apartments at the upper executive end
of the scale, and no earthly sign of *Dorothy*, though
the pipes continue to knock in that odd—annoying way.

DIRECTOR'S CUT

The director doesn't give a fig for the flat terrain
that pans the horizon; high heels make little impression
out here, her steps lightsome in this blazing void,
elegant calf muscles, sitting legs akimbo, a gangster's
mole abandoned to the *Badlands*, out of tune within
this harshness—high cheek bones aglow, radiant
and sweatless, the landscape set back from her Vegas

body, a hip thrust defiantly at the brighter than neon
sun. 'Cut!' he shouts through cupped hands that sound
hollow as a tin can out here. Her arm drops languid
at her side, too heavy for boredom, she waits to be made
over and makes for the caravan. The film guys give
way to the riggers and construction crew, a dreary day's
schedule, the pneumatic drill rears up and resumes

its place in the pecking order, mechanical and yellow.
Bright orange jackets under bright white helmets—
a wound, tricky as salt, appears alongside the new light
rail works. Did the first assistant producer make off
with the second? Ask Red, but he walked out yesterday.
Melanie fudged her lines the third day straight while
the backup generator got the stutters. No way out

of here for three weeks, he walked off into the desert,
but who knows? Nights passed cool though bugs rushed
the lanterns and the beer stayed cold, stars piled up
in a low budget sky. Sometime after, with the railway
platform finished, out came the Winchesters, we hollered
and hooted like old time pioneers, like celebrities at
The Charlton Heston Golden Gun Anniversary Awards.

THE WOOLSHED

I came upon it by a clough in the
hill, an involuntary turn upland, wheels
holding to the rub of an old bullock
track, by backblocks and tableland,

to unminded paddocks. A kennel whiff
of the grease curled fleece, flumped
on long benches in a low slung woolshed,
the fangled wool press fallen into

wrack and ruin, the dust, grease coated
floor planks. A sense of something slowly
tossed aside. And wind, the sound
rusty and hollow, breathed down the chute to
an empty holding pen, thickened with
dock weed, purpled in *Paterson's curse*.

BRADY'S GRAVE

'Listen to the moaning of the pine
at whose root thy hut is fastened'
          —Old Danish proverb

In front of the old Manse,
Duck Creek weaves through
bulrushes along the hillside
striving with pine trees,
slippery with copper needles

home to magpie's carolling.
'There were three homes we had.'
Farther back into the hill,
a tilted slab of concrete, rusty
iron posts and chains mark it out

amongst the tussock clumps—
Brady's Grave makes a slipway
for the flying, full moon;
and the local cats gather into
a circle, under the yellow glare.

A questioning silhouette
of *Black Swans at Pāuatahanui*
ride easy, buoyant, on the inlet's
long tides away from view,
behind the whistling pine grove.

WOLFHOUND CENTURY

after Osip Mandelstam

So by now you know it is time
to leave, they have damaged the name
of the city and time itself is imperilled;
clocktowers stand by snow-capped

and the hands splay crucified but
this is no bridge to safety. St Petersburg
[Petropolis] winds down gradually,
shifts the granite block of night back

from the tomb so dawn may enter in;
places a small saucer of daylight to bath
the eye. What sleds are heaped with
we cannot tell, but it is not the jubilation

of children's cries—at the sight of
the hill our hands drop to our sides black
as fence posts. God himself rubs his hands
at sunset but you cannot get warm.

October 10, 2000

AN ACTUAL ENCOUNTER WITH THE SUN
       ON MY BALCONY AT FRANCE STREET

When the moon slipped its knot
and left a ring for the night to drop
through, and a baggage of stars
thudded on the loading bay
at the other side of the world,

                                    I heard,
'Ho! get up you slack arse poet,
I want to have a word with you.'

            It was the sun.

'This is a surprise,' I yawned.

'Shouldn't be—you're the one whose
been whingeing about his own personal light.'

            'I must admit,' I conceded, *'I
was worried there for a bit.'*

                  'Right,' answered
the sun. He spat at the window turning
it molten.

'You must know by now Stephen,
I visit with a poet every thirty years or so.
Last time it was Frank O'Hara,

                        and before that,
Mayakovsky. Can't say it's your turn
but I'll stop by anyway.

You're not a poet for all time but
for your own time. Don't worry about it.

And forget those supposed poets
the *M=E=Z=Z=A=N=I=N=E=S* as you call them

caught between the floors: they ain't going
nowhere.

So get up and make a cup of tea!'

'Sure, care to join me?'

'Only for a minute,' he said, 'I've got more
important things to do today, like glinting
off the Hauraki Gulf and the ironclad poppy
of Centre Point Tower.

Oh, that reminds me,
then I'm off to San Francisco to wake up that
ex-girlfriend of yours you keep pissing
off with late night calls and false promises.'

By now I could
see the sun was pretty worked up.

'C'mon, forget that crap.
You write some good stuff but you've got to
hang in there, and like me it'll
come to light.'

'Thanks sun.'

'And knock off the guilt trips and stop
getting pissed (in your Sydney dreams, pal!) you'll
burn yourself out—I recognise the signs.'

*'Yeah, seems I have been
a little preoccupied.'*

       The sun jumped onto my balcony
outside the window.
'You don't see much of me down here at
POETS' PALACE—do you?

Move over,
this is the only time I get a look in.'

       I propped myself up
on one elbow.

       'Remember, you're not
writing bus timetables and calling it
"performance poetry" like a few I
could name. Stick with the atmospherics,
the true essence of people.

That's your angle, as mine is now
to brow-beat you.

And don't get into this doomsday kick
either, leave such things to the small minded.

       Honestly,
it's straight forward focus.'

       By now my hangover had
evaporated.

       *'Hold on sun,
I've a few questions.'*

'Sorry,' called the sun, receding.

'We've had our little talk. Give my regards

to Greece again, if you ever get there.'

   And he was gone
         and I got up to
another beginning, and a day.

BALLAD OF WITTY TICCY RAY

Excuse me one tic or two
I'm by far speedier than you
with a song or ping-pong.

Give me a multiple drum kit
you've never seen the likes of it—
extemporization and speed.

I can be loud or obscene
pitch a blood-curdling scream
it's neither here nor there.

I'm excessively excited
been said I'm much blighted
better that than slow.

Allow me one tic please
I can't imagine a life of ease
with Tourette Syndrome.

Mid-tic I've been caught
as if blinded on fortified port
blame that drug—*Haldol.*

How I love things that spin
a revolving door a garbage bin
I dodge quick as lightning.

I don't care for catatonia
and forget that sloth dystonia
it leaves me cold as jelly.

I'm a singular man—*a ticqueur*—
and there's no sure cure
from this glitch in the thalamus.

I'm the funniest man in town
call me *Ticcy Ray Tourette Clown*
yet I'm always sure to win.

Should a doctor wish to fix me
I would complain oh most wittily
then bounce him out the door.

SYDNEY BELLS

Gays go up and gays go down
to ring the bells of Sydney town.

Suspenders and tarts,
say the bells of St Mark's.

Zip up your flies,
say the bells at St Ives.

Pants full of piles,
say the bells at St Giles.

No worries mate,
say the bells at Ramsgate.

No drinks to minors,
say the bells of Maria Regina's.

Pots of old paints,
say the bells of All Saints.

A joint and champagne,
say the bells at Balmain.

Politicians and hat tricks,
say the bells at St Patrick's.

Sausages in batter,
say the bells at Parramatta.

Bimbos bring hassles,
say the bells of St Basil's.

A turd in your eye,
say the bright bells at Bondi.

I've got a court date,
say the bells at Mortlake.

Marriage banns?
say the bells of St Anne's.

Can't pay my tax fee,
bang the bells at Bexley.

Go broke on *New Start*,
loll the Bells of Leichhardt.

Who's at the door?
say the bells at Enmore.

Here comes a taxi to take you home,
and here comes a train to grind you to bone.

SKYE DOG

*'Description of a prominent literary critic:
he wanted to write poetry and ended up with
seven jobs'*—W.H. Auden

I am a shaggy Skye terrier
with a bark like a parson on heat,
I'd brown nose a copper's wife
or whatever it takes to get meat.

Be it Penguin or Puffin
it makes little difference to me,
I grab them by the tail feathers
and climb up them like a tree.

I am a scavenger by trade
there's no two ways about it;
I favour those who pat my nose
and bite those who smack it.

My back yard's what I know
I run round it twice a day,
but still I cannot catch my tail
nor chase those fleas away.

I sniff into old newspapers
(inky smells don't get me off)
for dirty deeds in book reviews;
I take my place at the trough.

A dog's life is subservient
he answers to his master's voice;
to lick his arse on demand
gets me the bone of my choice.

I am a shaggy Skye terrier
I bark at this and I bark at that,
whatever side of the fence I'm on
I follow the leader of the pack.

ONE NIGHT AT THE DUKE c. 1969

'One of those old-type natural fouled-up guys'
        —Philip Larkin

Cochrane had been ensconced for
at least a year—well on the way to a 25 yr.
bender. I had yet to vault the bar,
grab a bottle of *anything* off the shelf

in an act of bravado—*Māori Johnny,*
Cookie, Kennedy, Girvan—the regulars
and the drifters. Brian Bell already a
'legend' monstered *Radio NZ News* with

paranoid phone calls, verbally molested
women, then in tow with *Dun Mihaka*—the
Māori activist (who bared his arse
to the Queen) a brief, obscure collusion.

A couple of white thugs entered the
Public Bar, stood at distance—waiting, Dun
excused himself to either beat up, or
be beaten up, gone for the rest of the night.

Later, at a post-pub party in Kelburn,
Brian bailed up some woman in the kitchen,
shouting, *'I've sucked them off, yes! I've*
licked them off, yes! sucked them off ...'

over and over, demonic—by design;
agent provocateur. She stood her ground,
unfazed and impressive. Years later, I saw
Brian, out of his environment, at a

Globe Tavern poetry reading—run by
Dave Mitchell. A voice from up back of the
bar, *'I used to be a masturbator in Eketāhuna,
until I discovered Hugh Hefner,'* he

announced, *apropos* of nothing. I laughed.
No one else did. Mitchell glowered.
Who *you* turned the tables on is anyone's guess—
as a kid growing up in Palmerston North,

you made your own explosives, blew up
neighbour's back sheds—known at school as 'Dr
Stinky'—tall tales and true from the legendary
past; *eh Brian?* A boy's own sexuality

that extended into adulthood—rumours,
(as shift worker at *Tokoroa Paper Mills* in the
early '50s) of your sexual involvement
with a couple of bearded, Canadian loggers … *

You latched onto the literary and literate,
rode the gravy train where it took you, foxy eyes
darting—the mad mind of an anarchist,
amoral jester, fantasist, accidental *littérateur*.

Arch opportunist. Already, way outdated by
the time the '60s came round. For all that *fearless*,
beaten up in pubs by rugby players, bloodied,
leering like a ferret. Teeth bared: back for more.

June 5, 2003

**A tale related to me by the playwright/poet, Warren Dibble (1931-2014)
who first met Brian Bell (1929-2000) on the night shift at the Tokoroa Paper
Mills in the early '50s, and who witnessed, firsthand, Bell's priapic cavorting
with the aforementioned Canuck loggers.*

DEADLY POLLEN

You return to the *stupa*, yearly,
to seek your return. You wish to
come back as forest deer but
that deer is extinct. The stupa is a rock
upon which your dreams founder,
yearly—you return that which
you do not have. Meanwhile, in the
West, under ragged skies and beneath a
hundred spires no longer dreamt of—
attendance comes tumbling down;
each stone, unturned, in an emptied
space within a space caved under.

'With digital, there is no past,'
says Jean-Luc Godard. Either way,
the button is redundant. Voice command
is thought—the fear deep and futureless
as history, desire to appease which
remains featureless, not the disorganized
weather it truly is, as much a part of
the breathing stars as constancy of rock.
The 'Mr Whippy Man' weaves
Greensleeves in and out of suburbia; a
caravan in search of a trade route—
via the village that never existed.

How is it the floating island
detaches itself from horizon in dream—
its first appearance, otherworldly,
but of this world, a wheel loosened
from the world's ratchet, out of time,
riding above it and inhabited by
folk fixated upon a particular

theorem-thought; elevated imponderables,
whereby you access this island by door
set underneath as you sail under?
Islands, a dream of round towers!
The sudden rush of water under hulls.

Hugely, our indifference squats—
unleavened as fear, blood is contained
within news footage. Archaeologists
stop digging deserts because of
landmines. Camels wait for sand dunes
to drift into ridges—blue flags flutter
back at *Fort Apache* on brave
white trucks (what gets through
is the scent of coffee). A footless boy
hobbles past, bargain hunting,
a life at odds and ends—smoke drifts
over Manhattan, out across the Hudson
River as from a Bedouin campfire.

If streets had cobblestones
blood would flow in tatters—torn
flags to a revolution lost. Streets
smoothly ease to drains. The cut deep,
and blood wakes from its blackness,
crushed as berries in the runnels
of a wagon, oozes its oil from
the body's casket—till flesh becomes
porcelain, perfect surface for moon,
ice, the glass edged sky to play upon;
in silences deep as birch in the
bayoneting dark—and leaves finally
resemble paper money piled up
under the turbaned lamplight.

A Public Works draughtsman
spent thirty years designing the City
Sewerage Reticulation System
he eventually hoped to escape through—
a masterpiece! A prairie dog would
have been proud of it. Complex of
accented runs, angles, drops, sluices,
pumps, ditches, endless unbowed
archways, treatment ponds breaking into
sunlight—the architects of Athens
would have been proud of it.
Only on paper—not one trowel lifted!
Miles and miles and miles of it.

Pyrrha, your dewy hair,
yellow, scented, doubly wreathed
in Jasmine, fresh from the trellis
this morning—your new lover yet to
arrive, breathless. Your tantrums
are as sea storms, heart wrecking
for that unsuspecting voyager—maybe
as survivor, I might warn him
against your squally lust, he won't
find safe haven in your arms! This note
is record enough—that I set down
against your lubricious hold.

See: Horace's 'Pyrrha' ode. I,v.

Once cradle of civilization—
now crucible, a sandstorm of tanks,
a battery of rocket launchers
each one bright as a guiding star
slams home to its birthplace, sand sprites
leap dervishly, limbs gad about,
horses buckle back upon themselves—

empty out like exhausted bellows.
A beggar (in nameless rags) calls
out in either prayer or curse to
the desert night first refuge for saints;
Cross and Crescent belch fire.

A *giallo antico* moon framed
within cratered ruins. Country turned
up at the edges like a dirty postcard.
Poplars, broken spars of pine,
cypress. Dusty plane trees rubbed raw
by abrading tanks in the market
square. Two ambulances shoved aside.
Kabul. The Republic of Georgia's
snowy mountains, backdrop to some
desolate soccer field. A few lean
men shouldering grenade launchers pass
by and grin, heading for the glacière.

*'A line is taking a full-stop
for a walk,'* said Klee. A straight
line is the supreme act of cruelty;
is intent without reprieve, ambush
and final judgement; Alpha
and Omega, the beginning and end,
(bullet-to-victim), the scroll of
credits, a squadron of lines;
the banding of speech, a geology
of sound; the blade tilt of horizon
that bloodies a sun; is gravity
compressed and a disk flung wide,
is flatness departing life to nothing—
spear cast on a plain at sunset.

CEOs in castles cascade
in cash, silent as a cyber virus—
the invisible hides *cause-and-effect*,
stock taken, bartered in Japan—
via Belarus every back yard where
falls a city's shadow looming
over the last, dead chimney pot,
not even moon can empty its
chamber pot of yellow, silver slops
into alleyways crackling with
plastic syringes, used condoms,
blood trails, slewed off into a
wilderness of freeways, high-rise.
O the dead arise in elevators nightly
as Pharisees burst into the Temple.

So. Earth's most dramatic
'bald spot' (ozone hole) is down
to 15 million sq miles over
Antarctica as of Oct, 2002. Shrinkage,
Big Time. One year's reading on
reduced *cfcs* doth not a trend make.
Is this happy hour? Fewer recalcitrants
maced? Hair Gel instead of hair
spray? Asthmatic winds rake pebbles
in dry Arctic valleys. Presidents
and dictators square off. *Puritanism
v Tribalism*. Doomsday's a
syndicated affair. *Life's Good*.

I wanted to reach my hand into
the side of that mountain.
The Romans waited, the Jews died.
Made a sacrificial altar,
such as Abraham had to his God.
A small cave, pocketed at the

base of Masada. *Better death than
surrender*—a courageous act
for living against the odds. Day
by day danger renews, retribution
neither diminishes nor goes
away. To every Age a new generation,
bigger weapons to sound the void.

Alcatraz not Minoan ruins.
Morning mist hangs its garden off
Golden Gate Bridge. Men in
fog loom large. Fog or ram's horn?
Container ship—warrior barge,
passes under with another load of
Japanese cars to feast upon
freeways. *'Straight guys are at a
premium'* you said. (Or so I
overheard). Seven months under
your roof in your bed. I never got
to Texas—never hit *Route 66*.
Marooned on my isle, deep within
that lustful, solitary confinement.

EITHER SIDE THE HORIZON

LETTER TO AN ASTRONOMER

> *'Starry amorist, starward gone'*
> —Francis Thompson

Make no mistake—we arrived here first, by pathways
mostly forgotten, hinted at maybe, in the clinging moss on
gutter and drain, by ruined foundations, under destroyed
civilizations. Look no more, we are the visitors we
seek come via starburst and interstellar dust, riding the cold
chariots of comets, destined to make the biggest splash:
hominid, Neanderthal, Homo sapiens sought to track back
to what 'Courtyard of the Gods', multiple or singular,
in search of the primal spark, can hardly be guessed at.
Our breath might be read within the banded spectrum
of your inquiry that magnifies the sky's falling domino;
by wingbeat of light fleeing across the great glass lens.

Looking down through the whirligig
                           of immeasurable galaxies

will lead back again to the filmic awe over the retina as
you seek to locate by the interstices of deep space an echo
in nothingness. Granaries of knowledge (gravity's burden)
we laid down in ancient geologies; when we rested,
cities rose, when we walked, cities fell. Make no mistake
there'll be neither alien ship nor coded message exchanged,
merely (coming in under radar) signs of our passing
in time, most fluid of inventions—condemned forever to
rush forward, condemned forever to rush backward.
The orchard is rotten, the field beyond, cloaked in the
dandelion or wildflower waits for the plough or the sword.
Memory's digital code recounts something discarded,
as though God looked away for an instant after creation
and like uncertain visitors we fled from his hand as we fell.

January 14, 2000

TRUE NORTH

I

Here, to say North demands an extensive round
    of travel, first in mind, toward the sweaty gusset
of the tropics, volcanic soils, clarty and awash,
    caked roads, flannelette leaves, tyres growing in
circumference with every mile until jauntily stuck
    fast; beyond the whole thermos flask of S.E.
Asia, India and the Himalayas, further on to the grey
    slate plateaux of Afghanistan and the quarried
reefs of lapis lazuli, before you can entertain
    the snoring sound North makes at the roof of the
mouth, North as they would from Italy onward;
    North, that is, Sweden, Denmark, Finland, Norway,
Greenland; North, and finally the birch forests
    rugging off to an indefinite horizon over the tundra;
certainly not *Larkin's* North (O love blind as snow!)
    but someplace else, the indeterminate hyperborean,
beyond the north wind to the Arctic Circle where
    lights warble like organ music or taper piously,
the lights that lift the air into curtains and grottos
    and the narwhal slowly materializes on the photo plate
of ice, a ghost snapped in an extremely cold room,
    and the merest breath a bold statement of the living.

II

Here, to say North demands a dismissive outlook—
    beautiful one day, a developer's dream-text the next,
a mirage from Morocco, waves a curl of bank notes.
    The Gold Coast, the Sunshine Coast, the Great
South Coast Conurbation, surf club to surf club,
    running 2000 km of coastal veranda from cane
fields to pineapple plantations, this land is your land,
    this land is my land, from Cape York Peninsula
to the Great Australian Bight under one law white

as wave crests under a sky blue as a swimming pool.
(First destroy the sea-grass, then destroy the dugong).
   North, traveller—to Bali or Jakarta, Bangkok or
Rangoon, Malaysia and Singapore, to catch the Asian
   Tiger by the tail does not require following in
the steps of Buddha or Muhammad, only the shinning
   path of American Express and trade envoys in
Hilton foyers; *North*, past French Colonial Villas
   and trading posts from pre-Second-World-War novels;
until your steps lead you to a first flurry of snow flakes
   whirling like helicopter blades out of the Kashmir
valley where avalanches and guns, not cow bells,
   are the most ancient sounds to reach the western ear.

III

Here, to say North still holds magnetically true as
   the needle dips vertically to lodestone or mountain;
the packet boat three weeks overdue, bearers long
   gone, the company agent, oleaginous, first met on
the dockside (expansive now deferential) rarely
   seen outside the custom house or seedy rum saloon;
North, but not to *Nunavut*, and word arrives from
   the interior that the roads are near impassable, the
telegraph wires are down, either through flood, or
   activity of bandits moving up to limestone country.
Yet our man from Mogadishu was expected by
   the next full moon, catching dry winds off Oman;
we would recognise him by the yellow lateen sails
   of a felucca off the headland at this appointed hour.
Even the contrary winds that day fashioned an
   insignia in the sky—for a moment out of the North—
a drone of engines in close formation under cloud
   should have been headed elsewhere (the theatre of
war some leagues distant) for surely we would
   have known, our orders changed at the slightest hint?
As to the survey party, not so much as one word,
   getting lost up *Dolores Gorge* was wholly absurd.

NOIR

Or a light soft as yellow smoke playing about the silvery ruins,

    running over the archways,

where the archway might have been a 'sooty shadow' and the

    barn owl looking for a barn makes a

curtain rustling sound under the western wall and those scraps of

    night all quiet is a rubble of old movies

and the anonymous blonde who disappeared into the cellar to

    hurriedly search amongst brick

cavities for a cloth wrapped object *(never identified)* found herself

    a scuffled death, silent or muted,

recalls a walk off part her character left laid low, mortally coiled.

    Unreachable age,

where the smart kid sidles up to the car and gabs with the reporter

    'Got two-bob, mister?'

is a role that you were alive to play in way back then although

    never remembered,

which qualifies as dream uncomfortable as a consciousness that

     has outgrown life lived

as spectacle under the mottled light beam to applaud 20th century

     Fox amongst the palms and arc lights:

'O Californian mysteries'. Meanwhile, the Studebaker cushions

     the corner and turns

faster than the dolly tracking this scene and passes low down along

     the front row seats and idles sweetly,

segues the curb at last, comfortable as a cliché, and that pair of legs

     you're left to hope against hope

for again step out to savvy the sidewalk. Intellect takes a holiday,

     senses settle down to view

bleak perspectives over unfulfilled hours by which one means where

     one is, the old familiar address of self,

when the melancholy bout from heaven falls, glut it on a rose

     over the Spanish Steps the wraith of

John Keats sells gewgaws to open-mouthed tourists whose empty

     exclamations like ticker tape

rise into the air as plainsong. And yet, tradition still holds the

secret or sacred alliance

within the twin abstract conceits of 'gentleman' and 'art' when one

considers (say) Dirk Bogarde in

The Singer Not The Song who might have played the imperfect

Lord Byron so perfectly but didn't.

The is the Age of Opportunists that values cunning over grace as

all the dreaded cards foretold,

is a ruination greater than any loss borne—a declining sun enlarges

the lengthening shadows as

sunset falls off to the right (regular as clockwork) and plays out

like an endless, last supper.

In the beginning globalization and the world was one: O pray then

a return to city-safe pollution,

quarantined away from cringing forests the floating contours of

limestone hills

where bats straggle starlight mobile as any species-hopping virus to

brush chicken farm and piggery

over the Malaysia countryside hung bright as tropical tapestry.

Too late for prophecy

in the crowded currents, the tortured city intersections, electronic

       highways, genetic engineering,

and in the extirpation of allegory, where the unicorn has turned

       to obsidian in the corporate

laboratories, and to date the scientific legislators have found that

       'there ain't no cure for love'

and no matter who you ask directions of the journey back to Eden

       begins tomorrow.

The search is on for new creation myths in the light of the earlier,

       overly researched ones as

the hot issue under discussion in cabinets and war rooms revolves

       around whether the quotient on

Good & Evil since the beginning of time has increased / decreased

       in the proud light or remains

A Constant: is unanswerable in the studio warehouses of Foxtel

       by Sydney's revolving soundstage

or at the spooky boardrooms *via* Bill Gates' compound bluely squat

       on the Seattle harbour hills.

•

St. Teresa of Ávila, Julian of Norwich, St. John of the Cross, in the

back lot playing pétanque;

O Meister Eckhart, dream me a dream, Meister Eckhart, you from

whom God hid nothing—

does the true visionary stare down the endless tunnel of futility toward

His Light or the Will's supremacy?

King Cormac sharpens his sword on a granite outcrop at the palace

of Tara on the morning of December 5,

240 AD and thinks on his progeny and I stepping aboard a train city bound

at this millennium's close see him,

foot braced against rock and hear the Gadhelic blade sing in sunlight,

'be a listener in woods, a gazer at stars'

knows a bitter wind in the night will toss the ocean's white hair

bring the fierce warriors of Norway;

and William Carlos Williams who makes a storm out at sea makes

it bloom and hears it fade,

a flowery thing, rain scented, throughout the whole wide sea,

and in all its petalled gardens—

oompah goes old Europe under used up cigarette smoke *oompah*, sorrow, subtlety, love, loss.

Three eurodollars in a fountain and a brass band plays public gardens

    as soft grey stones prop up old stories

and cloud pulls its cloth cap down over the brow of a farmyard moon

    by a pitchfork stand of elm.

Eternal blackness, the God in the director's chair shouted *'action!'*

    then a billion lights came on,

the circuitry of the God's anger blew and lit a warehouse of galaxies

    'oh, what a feeling!'

Opening night in paradise a story line for every bad marriage to come

    laid out from playpen to military

campaign through watery ravines to tableland and far desert plateaux

    in banquet hall and wattle and daub huts.

Family slaughter is history shadow play back lit before a backdrop

    of burning city or blackened palisade—

Eden, the ultimate *Green Room*, antechamber to the God's high seat

    as godless poets called on God O.

Extinction or out-take, the director's cut on species / rushes thrown

    to the cutting room floor,

a recall to the factory though the flaw lay in the original design

     and not the bright prototype,

while damage control dictates that one sea horse put in a breeding tank

     does not a species make/re-make:

today we have naming of parts, yesterday we had biological safari,

     but today we have naming of parts as

coral glistens bleached white and imperial in all the neighbouring oceans,

     that point of balance we have not got.

        •

Don't trust the '90s man who whistles in the dark whistling up the

     wind is stalker or psychopath

no longer the friendly bobby of Dockside Green, nor the ploughman

     homeward plodding his weary way,

but the late night suited android outside in the galleria or parking

     lot by the dumpsters, the oily

dark of the freeway flexing out of the city into lurid billboards homey

     as motels down off ramps moving

parallel brushing by his shoulder cruising vacant as a Jeffrey Smart

      urban landscape and suddenly is there

looming dead still, dead quiet, fixedly stands before you the breathy

      whistler, the suited android.

In your mind you are the kid again back by the bus stop waiting

      on your father (responsible yet) to

collect you from the green dental building with rows of globed lights

      numbered and nursed

the stranger threatening with a bag of sweets to whisk you away in his

      car hidden close by and you unsafe on

Willis Street that is by far too wide, open to hide your fear in where

      the lolly pop sun melts down

and you crinkle your face up hopefully into a protective tough mask

      older kids wear against their own because

the surprised, wide-eyed approach fell back to likely encouragement

      as the man with sweets cruised by again.

Can you remember what you felt then? Loss of confidence in dealing

      with authority and a later life,

here you first suspected corruption without knowing its true name;

a bogus kindness, trick, or vulnerability.

Can you remember what you saw then? The regular Saturday matinee

echoing footsteps at the core of light

into the darkened room steps the villain invisible with *unhurrying*

chase, and unperturbèd pace—

you followed the perils of the man who walked the shaft of light faded

into an immovable, black space.

Newsreel footage: crowds, trees struck in surprise of autumn, flags;

parachutists blister sky over Normandy;

match flare on horizon from *USS Missouri*; atom bomb uncorks a cloud;

camera flashes cup winner;

God saved the Queen save us every Saturday arvo with *Looney Tunes*

flicks at the Brooklyn 'flea-house'.

Clint Walker looming large in buckskin through mountain torrent

and conifer in *Night Of The Grizzly*;

Jeff Chandler, steel grey-haired on the bridge of the battleship doing

it tough under Jap zeros;

ghost of Doris Day (bright as a haystack) Elvis, gangsters and Apaches,

    an iris opening on mesa country.

•

Old curled, black and white beach shots, the shore line rocks blurred,

    an opaque sea and one young parent,

you out of shot (in memory) long before puberty had landed with its

    civilizing, cinematic angst—

Save the little Angel in the arch, that marble lintel fallen into the alley

    (say) a small collapse in Venice

a daily event important as prayer or washing hung out on balconies

    where floods rise in drains over

St. Mark's Square, that you wonder if Venice will blur, Turneresque

    to memory? Golden city of the lagoons

its foundations sunk 12 to 25 cm since 1900 still within view of the oil

    refinery and tankers that ply

mainland channels and giant cruise ships tower above San Marco ever

    deeper channels and draughts

open the city to Adriatic flood tides as authorities debate lock structures

or mobile barriers and the Italia Nostra weeps

not for Visconti's but another environmental death threatening Venice

a plague of speed boats and oil tankers

the slow disintegration of the platonic ideal into age, death and decay

styled as sensuality—

O applaud again Dirk Bogarde's poise (repeated in *The Night Porter*)

a childhood turned nightmare

garish as fever or the devil's harlequin laughing madly at the hotel guests,

he saw the demon floating

out of his body the condemned man embracing a barren, last yearning

in the last days of that century,

in the last wash of light, the impossibly sad flow of Mahler's farewell at

the borderless regions of dream.

Dawn, no hasty orisons nor nom de guerre for tribes out of Africa,

from first light to campfire lit

over unacknowledged distances, quicker than continental drift, arose

the technomadic culture

the 'hunters & gatherers' v the 'fitters & turners' guided by the noetic

    compass, under ridged brows

that served as caves of thought, they paused, and man who paused

    long enough to reflect on his

going hence as his coming hither, made of stars an inkling unto history

    writ in every print (since made

or observed) later preserved in magnetic circle and the runic signal,

    while every leave-taking

became a yearning, simple as a hut, safe as houses, heard solid as speech;

    still later—ritual fixed its bayonet

and fire that bounced off the wall of dark, twined and interlocked demons,

    and it was demons made speech—

the castle instructed found the city as the river encircled became a moat,

    thinking man walked and made the road.

As through a telescope (winkle of light at the bottom of the well) by

    day you recalled children's voices

off the island loud as gulls, here it is a nightly wind brings grandeur

    to the least of cities,

and enlarges—high up on rock strewn ground monks pass under flared

stars, welts of light in the sky's arc,

to the Byzantine chapel overlooking the sea, a glistening darkness,

to this small, high interior, soft lit

that is memory of all caves that gathered diverging tribes over time

and before time when roaring

dissension from out every era closed, passed, and dimmed, heard in

chants rubbed vocally by antiphon;

echoes departing into whispering that leave in single file once more

out across the mountain pathways.

At the height of the winter solstice, the sun's longest rays between

the trilithon in low shimmering,

golden planks fall to the stone altars of the dead laid deep in barrows;

the soul is grown wise in the dark,

yearns to return to the light, again to enliven all growing things.

Generosity of infinity

is a question of silence moved and steadied by the layers of night on

this winter solstice, here contained

within the stone's ribcage, allows spirit and breath to brighten blood-red,

    remembered as the

dizzying motes of stars at Stonehenge on the Salisbury Plain encircled.

    Annex or vestibule

serve as always, departure points of the compass, a corridor placed

    parallel to our time, waiting room,

lit chamber at Newgrange no longer Vox Stellarum of ancestral spirits

    who never looked back

as we do to a belonging (at once the simultaneous defeat of time) when

    every way lay open—

texture of stone, sacred and upright, arranged through us by them stands

    attendant upon our seeing

and our dreams, knowing that is an unknowing, eternally present,

    played out over the ruined senses.

Winter solstice/21 December, 1999

1979 / A FLIGHT

'I dreamed of 747s over geometric farms"
        —Joni Mitchell/Amelia

At this altitude, ascending and moments later,
smooth as butter, another community folds beneath an
undulating, perfectly focused chessboard of canola,

across sorghum and furrowed paddock, flying
through cloud print or shadow rush, the ploughshare
wing that scythes and harries farmland, then banks

out over grey-blue ocean to hold above cloud;
the tables turned on day and night a traveller imagines
as either lost behind or forward ravelling distant.

Sometime later, campfire and tents, stamped
hexagonally into darkness below that confines Istanbul—
are lights that phosphoresce out under the fuselage;

like the green tossed flickering off the Red Sea
onto shores leading up to the Sinai Desert where dawn
finds pale jade lozenges left out upon those sands.

HANIA

Before the curvature of the quayside restaurants and bars.

You'd think the fishing boats had been brought in overnight
especially to set the scene for dawn over the Cretan port of Hania—

white, with yellow or red trim, all the tribal memories.
They jostle shoulders, low bellied, open armed, sleepily expectant.

Erase this scene, and the last thing to go would be the boats,
that and the Aegean taking its fill of bluestone light.

We sip coffee and sweet iced water at a café on the quay,
feeling the Metaxa pecking at our livers like an eagle from the

night before, and the night before that. The *Pirates Bar* awaits
the next night's big adventure where you shuffle sex like a bag full

of passports. What is it you expect as you follow the thread of
moonlight out over the old harbour? It's in the air all about you.

In another age you would have hoisted sail—advanced a thought.

Consider the *Lilies of the Field*. Amongst landmines in Afghanistan, Bosnia, Eritrea, Ethiopia, Mozambique, Angola, Cambodia, and Egypt—which tops the bill with twenty three million landmines. Wherever invading troops in retreat have left a tidal slick of bone fragment, gobbets of flesh, stumps that were once children, old men, women. Limbs vaporized.

Landmines Must Be Stopped campaigns the UN. A small girl in a bright dress picking up a shiny object. The dress made brighter. Consider the *Lilies of the Field*, the exploding blooms of landmines, so spectacularly undramatic, a muffled bang, a puff of smoke and dirt, from the safe distance of a news clip. Untidy air.

But on a winter's night, bare branches before a rushing sky. A turbulent moon. The earth smelling black, breathing, holding in these subcutaneous cysts, metal implants, each a footpad for the crazy dance of death. Millions of them (*est.* twenty years to clear at current rate) each with its own graven serial number, endlessly patient, waiting the impress of heel, or lightly shifting step.

This light over the land, made ancient by earlier habitations, wars, villages and migrations, dismantling through the hours and days, over long stretches of time; minefields—abandoned tracts of land. *The Lilies of the Field* so secure in their fate that every spring they bloom here, as though announcing entrance to the cemetery and under-world.

The hen is not so wise, nor *Zbigniew Herbert* skewered. Asbestos coloured, squat soldier of understorey and tree base, neurotic inhabitant of the tribal village, rhomboid citizen of backyards that no longer exist, behind hill-perched, stuccoed houses affronting panoramic harbour views. Zany monitor of daybreak, escapee to macrocarpa and rafter, beyond the precincts of wire netted fowl runs.

A squabble of hens is unparliamentary, a ruck and scrummage, an embodiment of what a crowd is; a potential riot. A motley of tribes and tongues, a disorder of nations, barrio and ghetto inhabitant. A bloom of feathers overriding reptile claws, milliner's folly, tavern sign, a disposition at odds with itself, grounded, clumsy amongst branches, its awareness a half-remembered flight. Avian refugee. Progenitor of griffin.

We are thus related to this fallibility—a half complete species; two parts absurdity, one part dream. Served up at an evolutionary banquet of invention and ferocious self-consumption.

What lies at the end of this petrol-hued rainbow, is an oil slick way out to sea, overarching proboscis sucking up light and colour into bands, into a glorious stain of creation. The refinery port of Botany Bay could be Piraeus, Jaffa or Tel Aviv. Flatland horizon, reminiscent of an earlier, grandfatherly generation.

Gasworks and pylons, steam trains chugging between the first and second world wars under sooty railway bridges, beneath a cloth cap sky. The pithead wheel stilled, the first and last grotto of the Industrial Revolution. In these narrow regions, asphalt fades grey in back streets, rail yards blur into rust and weed. Lime oxidizes in abandoned brick yards. The solitary coal stacks stand sentinel at dusk. The final, romantic tableau.

Summer is sustained, momentary, and present. Car sized concrete blocks pack the breakwater. White storage tanks glisten tidily, compose to view the fuel depot. Small waves dissolve into miniature cornices and cartouches upon the sand. Whittled light silvers the waters at Little Bay/La Perouse.

Sydney on a Tuesday morning, early September. Spring clangs in—Egyptian distances toward Botany Bay. Fuel haze and aircraft aswim. The season of *petro sunrises* begins. Birds study a new notation, a register higher. Suburban trees pay homage to buildings, puff into lantern green leaf and bud. Jasmine bloom wraiths a driveway, lays its scent over the boundary, tracking the pavement.

Word play between couples ease and relax, assured as an unfinished novel. Each heart a vignette. Speech not yet a song as eyes loft lightward. A clump of wind fusses amongst tree crowns, troubled stillness. A midden of pigeons rise and expand, shell bright against a white, backwash sky. Youth is green as an Elizabethan sward, laughter local as a hedgerow.

Garbage bins release their odours and overflow; little storage silos that make good pickings for the hunched vagrant, selective in the morning traffic, delicately fingering at elbow length breakfast discards. Street noise friable as asphalt. News bulletins rummage amongst the world's dross.

THE GREAT UNSAYING

Farther off, came lightning silent and unanswering,
the tower that emerged from between the flashes—solid
as an after-image, and then again, with each
intermittent opening out of darkness, the figure enlarged,
advanced, *message-bearer*, refugee from a tongue-
tied past, a bronze shield hanging off the darkened wrist.
He brought with him, and in the turbulence that
surrounded him, memories of words knotted along the
rope of language, the iron roar of the rabble rising
and falling, the flayed backs of the orators retreating.

Every portal round the tower consonantal, every window
an enjambment, the noise rose, a drowning roar—
unstoppable, even under the abstract gaze of the linguists;
voices shrieked back into primal colour—every
portal seemed a stopped up mouth that spiralled the honey-
combed tower; and this monument, curled into a ram's
horn became vortex and blasphemy. Temple or tower,
he lamented what once had stood shaped to cup hand
and mind holy as a grail. Only his closeness now fathomed
the air, tumbrels of boiling cloud carried the speech,
upon whose face contorted words, and every word a leech.

A SIMPLE TALE

*On the destruction of two giant, ancient Buddha statues, near
Bamiyan in central Afghanistan, by the Taliban militia in the
Year of Our Lord, March 12, 2001.*

In this stark country where light can be yellow
        it is difficult to measure time.

Bare mountains, seemingly carved, overlook
        ancient sea beds called deserts.

The Silk Road, or a tributary of it, drifted
        this way past the cliff face—

for a generation men on rickety scaffolding
        worked at the sandstone

to fashion the image deep into the cliff's face
        of a fifty metre high statue.

The mountain became grotto to the Buddha
        homaged by 1,700 years of dawns

and sunsets until the coming of the iconoclasts
        in a drought-stricken land.

In two unhurried afternoons, much like any other,
        between the braying of donkeys,

with mortar fire and dynamite, they turned to
        dust and rubble the false idol.

The last piece to dissolve before dusk which is
        the traditional time for prayer—

was the impassive smile of the Buddha, and 500
        tons of face fell under the blast.

THE GREY GLAS SONG

I am the cold watery current of the air,
I am the wreathing hand of mists,
I am the many-windowed firmament,
I am the coloured winds on the cloth of night,
I am the cloudy shell around the earth,
I am the four chief winds of creation,
I am the speckled winds riding the world,
I am the beaked-boat emerging at dawn,
I am the eight encircling servant winds,
I am a thousand lamps breaking in the wave,
I am the weight of a waterfall from a cliff,
I am the red plain of the earth at sunset,
I am the spear thrust of streams from a hill,
I am the lake bursting forth upon the plain,
I am the tall stones circled for strong memory.
Who counts the stars at the well's bottom?
Who is it follows the sun in his circuit?
Who is it keeps the sun fixed on his path?
Who thrice blesses the tides lifting and falling?
Who welcomes the morning of grey dews
knows fiery arrows pierce the breast for vision.
The poet's breath empties up into the night
who calls his answer across deep waves.

Tin goods sheds, the cantilevered skyline reconfigure throughout the day, the airport busy as a pavement. From here it's twenty four hours in the air to the Northern Hemisphere; older foundations, battle thick walls, multi-layered atmospheres, studded and embossed. One regime after another—history's gargantuan form from whose *'rybes they make bowes to shoot with'*. Sheep graze the old battlefields pretty as a picture, amongst the hawthorn and pylons.

Looking south toward Botany Bay, sinking beneath long rooflines, planes drift a bright tail fin along the east-west runway, or suddenly appear before you stuck on the sky like in a child's drawing, cushioned on volumes of engine roar, big colours loading the foreground, movement that is the elongated removal of time in the lifting sweep, diminuendo to a quiet speck, climbing out over the ocean—silvered shafts from a yeoman's bow falling far off to become traffic somewhere.

The mind says that memory is filtered through gauze. And immediately you are there. Banked up yellow soil-rubble along the coastline toward Jaffa port, fuel storage depot tabernacled in the Mediterranean light, winding through the dockside at Piraeus, (backstreets of Newtown reminiscent of *Ano Petralona*) and the air sweet with petroleum. The day shimmering in youthful heat.

The magnolia flower bruise-purple, cream cupped, under September. Long haul promise of summer heat and forests illuminated in scripts of flame, the sky's pinafore a blue, bleached out migraine.

The land insisting upon it's climactic heritage beyond the roar of air conditioning in a million suburban homes, within the short term memory loss of kitchen and living room; discrete zones for the petty crimes of the heart. Clearing rooms for hoarded angers given over to street cred.

Clouds troop from the southern horizon, lightning lays down its picket fence through the postal zones. *Hamid* pulls up alongside *Zang Wei* in the slow lane, and pumps a crescent of bullets into the driver's seat. Intersection lights-gone-yellow-gone-red-gone-green. High season of Taxi Wars along the Princes Highway. The Channel Ten Eye in the Sky helicopter reports traffic backed up to Bankstown.

Follow the metallic serpent with scales flashing back down Parramatta Road to Rockdale. Tomorrow a dawn of middle eastern appearance will rise over Newtown: Gateway to the East.

Sydney, September 10, 2002

If you do not remember yourself in death, mesmerized under the pendulum of that sea, would you care who remembered you after? The visionary demands absences. *Make it your own—you'll remember*. Give uncertainty name and form, fashioned after your inconsistencies, as the Ancients did to make their gods, or as the gods allowed them.

Power to destroy denotes an independent existence, the force to overrule breath, decides fate. So the mythic infrastructure was set in place and materialism became subservient to it. *Vision transmuted into form. Structure duly paid homage*. In time and beyond it, the idea predominated and became the absolute.

The argument: how to reconcile the gods with the one. This became the obelisk set in the technology landscape. Technological invention enveloped the globe in an artificial dimension. The elements of time and space cavorted in the re-enactment of the genesis principle. Chaos is the theory that insists creation equals destruction.

The philosopher's job is to record the progress of enlightenment syllogistically. The poet's job is to preserve memory under the articles of self-effacement.

A DREAM LIKE A TORN POSTER

The posse out to hunt down
God's kingdom,
                    hoofbeats respond to

the plains like shibboleth
and testing ground for those who

hear the coming of the Word.

Prayer is a vast silence that
follows hard upon an auto accident.

A breeze twitches in the joints
of trees, something scuttles through

the grass within earshot.

Arguments bunch and abound on
the horizon,
                    darkening the day's mood.

The moon barks its shins against
a tree stump.

Dugouts and trenches in cloudbanks,
a machinegun nest of lightning busies itself

in one corner of the sky—empty,
except for the blazed signature at dawn.

LAST THINGS

In this dream, you are on twilight
reconnaissance, the target not yet disclosed,
except for the moon, first coin of night,
that illuminates the wrecked flood plains
and difficult gorges. The river, weighty in its groove,
(sluggish as mercury) guides you back
toward the mountains. Peneus, an old god—
barks his shins on locks and dams.

Would you go back if you knew
what future lay before you; exuviae, triumphs
that pass as smoke over broken pedestals,
wash of ocean liners, afterburn of jets, crowd roar
always the same, a baying for blood,
conflict and allegiance; diminution of worldly
resources, cleared tracts of forest,
diminished birdsong, this world that lost its
memory in a progressive sickness—
once it had fully embraced the colloquial?

EASTERN SEABOARD, OCTOBER

Dusk, everyone and everything back to its
corner—a little Greek girl next door bounces a hug-sized
plastic ball on a terra-cotta patio, *coughs*,
but a child's cough sounds happily insincere and safe.
A myna bird guns it past the guttering into an
emerging pocket of shadowy tree.
Car boots close. Doors open. Car doors close, conclusively.
A uniform spill of thin dark washes out the sky,
a salute to the lights crackling across far suburbs. Sounds isolate.
Wind rattle in an old palm tree outside the converted
boarding house—multi-layered plane roar,
descending, the sound tired, and suddenly rush focused.
A train line busies and curves between stations—
invisible, comforting; *'freight train, freight train, goin' so fast'*,
not here though—this is not plains country
just an ancient river basin with a city circuit and tentacles
of inner harbour richly blue-grey,
fringed with swimming pools, bright as optics.

The new leafed camphor laurel, the hissing it makes as
night air stirs. Deep purple slate roofs part seen through branches.
Sydney awaits the solidungular pounding of summer heat
when it becomes an oven box (thickly humid)
though not as bad as Brisbane, frontier town to the tropics,
'beautiful one day, frivolous the next'.
A stillness everywhere. Intermittent scent of rain like the smell
off a lost paddock. A vertical uplifting of sky
and a darkening, an immediate future of thunder;
boulders rolled off a cliff top into the deep passes of the city.
Small moments of peace harboured between
indecision and the world's latest instalment of brinkmanship.
The Articles of Noise programmed to their targets along
the curve where discoveries once set sail.
A currawong the last inhabitant to leave the sky. Dark closes.

Lycanthropic cloud prowl, shaggy throated,
rummage amidst flight paths over the city, light smear,
and roar of metal overhead heading toward
Kingsford and Botany Bay. *'They get so close you can read
Dunlop on the tyres'*, said an acquaintance from
an earlier era, his voice itself one rigorous growl through
air waves when punk made the ghetto sound hip,
and Thatcher was a back room stooge made good, iron maiden,
a ball busting, union breaking bitch. Brief London days,
when I found myself one night in an abandoned
squat, fucking a spiky haired slag who squawked, *'try him,
he's pretty good'* to her 'timid as' girlfriend in
the wolverine flicker of street light. Like a lost B-grade flick,
the storm carries its rumour beyond regret,
nothing more than an untidiness of air, a contortion as in
a dream sizzling through this flash, angry hour.

Harrington Street, Enmore, Sydney, 2003

PŌHUTUKĀWA OF LA CORUÑA

'Wellington: *A pōhutukāwa tree in
Spain has stirred debate on whether
the Spanish were the first Europeans
to reach New Zealand'*
      —Sydney Morning Herald, *September 22–23, 2001*

Bark bearded, large as a mastodon, it
stands within its neat stone ring;
the pōhutukāwa at La Coruña, north western
Spain, capital of Galicia province,
(an early Celtic colony); memory growth five
hundred years back, hold secrets of
cartographers ornately in its curves; guessed
at trade routes branching Pacific latitudes,
El Dorado seen along the East coast
of Aotearoa—smoke moving behind olive
foliage off morning fires, smudged cove, inlet;
crowded pōhutukāwa bloom,
glowing with the first heat of iron that bleeds
heart red, out into the rising daylight.

MUNCH MUSEUM, OSLO

For the second time in a decade,
another version of Munch's 'The Scream'
has been stolen in broad daylight;
this time, two men in ski masks (one

waving a handgun) walked past
stunned viewers, up to *the 'oval mouthed*
man by the railings qua 'The Scream'
(in Oslo), tore the painting from its

wire moorings, got clean away via
a station wagon parked outside, bits of
frame strewn in their wake. 'The
Scream' represents loneliness, isolation,

despair, muted panic, the sort of panic
one would feel *drowning*. Who in their right
mind would live with such a painting, let
alone steal it; such despair is commonplace.

August 23, 2004

OCCUPATIONS

2.

Every night it is the same, greenly spun
in the iced cube light of skyscrapers, the Master
Chef dreams he is pitched from the highest
viewing deck in all the world: *Grollo Tower*,
down through boiling mist into the river Yarra.

5.

Nostalgia killed her, my mother, for the
Ireland she'd never seen—*that*, and the harsh
realities of family; a catholic cocktail, why
it sheared off into a broken dream, drunkenness,
children become Priests of the Pragmatic.

6.

Which way the *thylacine*: Tasmanian
tiger, Woodgate tiger, Ozenkadnook tiger, or
Cape Tribulation tiger? Whichever way, a
repeatedly brutish people; enthusiastic
practitioners of genocide and land degradation.

9.

You and me and sun on the roof caught
up in the stridulations of *greengrocers, red-eyes,*
black princes and *double-drummers,* from
suburban shires to watery reaches; tinder-dry
excitement before a bravura of bushfires.

13.

Flat as a postage stamp? Weather shall
age her through sandstone, back through time
older than any dream tale yet untold:
and rightly too claimed thus for all her mineral
worth, lest we forget, call her *Brownland.*

14.

Southern Ocean at 60° south, 100° east;
ice chambered blue, a deep radium allure.
Brash ice, weathered and glacial, herded by those
thousand year, kilometered, tabular bergs:
(*sérac*) the busted teeth of Antarctic Peninsula.

15.

This mountainous static heard at far
remove is tall sounding rain though conifer,
soft (through time and space sifted) from
Mount Stromlo, by way of stars, in hands held
open and sensitive as a satellite dish.

17.

A crossbow of lights. Irresolute sky.
The hour's gauze. A plane banks, turns east
out across the Timor Sea. Borneo caged in smoke.
An economy in tatters. After the burn offs,
the last orange-pelted wild man made extinct.

24.

They say, 'All grooves lead to NYC',
fluorescent floor racks, pixel cubes screened
in red, blue, yellow, apple green, whatever;
chrome assemblage of the Chrysler Building with
the slow, descending stylus of Brooklyn Bridge.

31.

Momentarily, from the eye's corner,
an aboriginal 'dot' painting, serpentine on a
concrete wall, but no; just a red and black
stripy tape against a building site—*oh*, something
that might cordon off the scene of a crime.

37.

At the National League's Bunyah charter,
the provost marshal presides and states the motto:
'fathers of the country, fathers of the future'—
see the creature that slopes toward Canberra!
See the shuffle of the wrong-footed people.

39.

The potter at his wheel echoes within
the hollow palm, spherical, the one furrowed,
turning line with a gesture that yokes:
from the rhyming hum in the ancient vase
the first known example of written verse.

43.

'Men like war and women like warriors'.'
War again, it's war once more, dear friends,
let the trumpets of cyber land glaze our screens!
Let the watch dog space monitors point a
destructive finger across God's dome pointedly.

47.

Orchid of Snow! Mount Taranaki prints against
a mackerel sky—at 30,000 feet, I head out over
pink wash of the Tasman from Auckland; streets
falling into phalanxes like sad pride, intense
anger, the last intersection out of a century's glare.

48.

Advance: O Let us boast a standard gauge,
one rail one nation; applaud a republic on track,
a history laid to rest optically; a white picket
fence for every home; a barcode for every
gene—the Blackfella Hall of Fame: *Australia*.

49.

Earth turns tight as a brake drum.
The moon blackens to full eclipse on Broken Hill;
hard hats glint in the opal light of the public
bar. Tomorrow, the moon will lie exhausted
and the night clear—bright as a billboard.

52.

In the dark, unbounded warehouse that
is nothingness, God snapped his fingers like a
match, the universe unfolded in the cup
of his hand to glow forever, fathomlessly, until
we saw by light leakage—it close to a fist.

53.

When they threw the breaker the powder
erupted Krakatau red on arch truss, hanger, the
Sydney Harbour Bridge. A coronet of white
sky rockets, spillage of chemical colour; $150,000
smoked out the old, welcomed in New *Yeah!*

55.

Hush! the quiet backwaters of Sydney's
south-western bays; Blackwattle, Rose, Iron Cove,
loud with the glow of heavy metal contaminants
from road run off into storm water drains:
O lead/zinc that irradiates harbour sediment.

60.

In that long room at the back of every
skull, Socrates and Jesus face off forever over
drinking vessels, each agreeably cognizant
of the toast, though each in his heart wishing the
contents of his cup belonged to the other.

65.

The night before she died, twelve year old
Nirvana danced and whirled her life to a sensuous
ghost, the following morning in the Sarajevo
market place, a mortar bomb exploded, and glass
severed the great irrigating vein of her neck.

66.

In Sarajevo the soccer fields are cemeteries,
teams of corpses represent most ethnic groupings;
equal in length, weight, decomposition, status,
terminal dates, forgotten applause, the crowd roar—
death is a tournament that plays all seasons.

69.

Without Dante, Chaucer, Shakespeare could
never have formalized the pagan mind to conquer
the Roman—réveillé for Pict, Celt and Saxon,
from whose shouted plunder he made of language
a bannered procession, of metaphor a trophy.

73.

Flat as corruption Melbourne dreams it's
Vienna (tired weather), intersection lights flash
who's who under foppish plane trees, poets
sashay back and forth from café to pub reading:
tidily languid in a 19th century sort of way.

76.

JOHN CLARE, you walked the eighty miles
from High Beach Asylum to where you believed
your 'wife' waited though dead, exhausted,
hallucinating, eating grass—yet the home you
sought was the idyll of an unfastened mind.

77.

All roads lead to Boot hill; all roads lead
to the charnel house; all roads lead to the bone
yard; down cemetery road literary guns from
the legendary past went herding a cumulus cloud:
Zane Grey, Hemingway and Roy Campbell.

78.

At Blackheath, lightning whangs onto the
escarpment like a hammer to anvil, substations
of cloud shorting out along the Great Dividing
Range, sheeting ravines and undiscovered foliage,
each airy gust packed as full as a warehouse.

80.

O how picturesque the country roads!
Village folk fleeing, bare trees, snow patches,
the wounded, the stragglers, children who
cry at mortar and tank fire—even refugees with
Adidas T-Shirts and runners die as quick.

89.

The storm withdrew from the French Alps
as a fist into its sleeve. Over four hunched months
behind these mountains, a sun cold as a hubcap;
in montane valleys rituals begin—religions,
the baking of bread, its smell become festival.

90.

The flood spoke volumes to Lake Eyre;
pelicans, water lily, all manner of water fowl—
4 wheel drives came to drink at the water's edge,
camera crew and sound men came to document
this inland body of water as if it were mirage!

91.

O Gothamite! a slave in NYC, you are
centrobaric to it, caught between the East River
and Westside, as clouds roll cotton bales over
Times Square, and tourists fall in where
once the English came but going—torched it.

94.

A cross is the brand on the hide of cattle,
it is a bombsight, it is the silhouette on a hill,
it is transept, it is a man standing before an horizon,
it is the world's navel, and the rim of the world,
it is the still point and equipoise of the wheel.

100.

This tropical vegetation as tossed salad:
under the clearing chains in Queensland 1.8
million hectares a year (the best went first) from
the good ship *Australis*, the rural hull breached;
a salt Plimsoll line encrusting this continent.

106.

There are many walls in Israel: The wailing
wall (yes!), settlement walls, electrical barbed wire
walls, ethnic and biblical walls, historical
precedent walls, them and us walls. All this done
in the name of dirt—*dirt is what you spit on*.

HARMONIC

AN AVENUE TO THE SEA

Knowledge comes by indirect paths,
found addresses, by moonlight's note left on the

back doorstep, molecular puzzle

of pigeons (brown and white potsherd)
in the high air at midday over this raucous town,

by panels of light cantilevered off cloud
that signal the departure of angels to earthly realms.

City of property investors, real estate mania.
City of rack-renters and home renovators.

City of bladed light and blue-grey harbour.
City of broken contracts and sybaritic compulsion.

City of up-front rip-offs and council rorts.
City of jasmine and the eternal summer party.

City of shimmer dreams-sans-memory.

The most famous of living poets remain anonymous
and unrecognized in foreign towns,
                    ghosts before their time.

An avenue of artists, philosophers, poets, musicians
leads from the city square out through suburbs,

past terra cotta, yellow, and liver-brick villas—
(smoke twists through pine and laurel grove)

an avenue wide enough for a phalanx of soldiers
or two tanks grazing side by side.

Flags of spiritual battles won and lost adorn poles
set at intervals, diminishing
                    whitely into distance,

where it is observed that a central point at the close
of the avenue, bright as diamonds streaming in

the light (barely larger than your pupil), is the
sea burning in its cauldron of watery fragmentation.

GOD OFF HIS BACK PORCH

'Globalization is Imperialism by email,'
says Arundhati Roy. 'Get rid of the Big Ideas,

the Big Lies ... the Big Dams ...'

Charles Wright celebrates what's seen off his back
porch, neighbours idling, dogwood bloom,

light stretching and contracting over Blue Ridge,
the opalescent brooch of sky pinned onto

night's lapel—each season's lovely,
renewed threat to mortality, maintains the Tradition

of Discovery, hears the small motors of the world

at work—whisper in the catacomb of the worm,
grass blade holding its hull to the turning earth—

he performs the secret ministry of the poet truly,
in the awed, low struck observations off his back porch,

sees the kingdoms of the earth spangled before him,
and performs his own spiritual

autopsy just as the Ancients saw it,

encoded deep in simplicity, a viewing platform
for what the eye discerns of wisdom in things passing—

as if vision were the gift borne of patience, assuming *Weltanschauung*
is a private worldview.

PHAETHON RIDES AGAIN

Welcome to this morning's minion, star bright
as a weather balloon, porcelain sky and mare's tail,
                gold bullion sunrise.

One ray's pre-emptive strike over my windowsill.

At 7 am the day has whitened—humidity 83%,
the bunched, iron fist of summer just round the corner.

Out of Botany Bay the roar of early morning flights,

(small flight of starlings ebullient in their own silent movie)
                tail fins slicing through haze

as in a medieval parade of pennants on manoeuvres—

destinations not so certain these days under
the high-risk factor of fear and political backwash.

Corporate leaders of the western world angling
for position, forecasting futures,
                soothsaying armies into position.

Deep yearning going/gone nowhere—
is a huge guilt shunting the present through history

landfilling the void.

We continue to fall over the
edge of the world even though we don't believe it,

that we are our own biggest ghosts, self-spooked.

8 am sees the last retreat of shadow from
suburban back yards—eastward, the sky asbestos
                    white as a mosque.

The first fiery thorns of day confirm that
though I yearn for dusk, it is unreachable, where

the crickets press doorbells into evening.

Then Phaethon in his panic dropped the reins
across the tinder haunches of the fleeing horses,

manes aflame, meteoric, chariot rampaging

the lower levels of heaven, wheels grinding
thick air to ember attack—helpless, and heading to

his reckless death, no longer defiant, flaming
                    out in terror as earth burned, rivers
and lakes, entire oceans steamed and shrank.

Stunned, the free-choosing gods
                    (known to cross-dress for seduction)
stood by helpless before the overriding blaze.

That self-same slap of reins is heard yet
                exploding fireballs

through bush in the Hunter Valley, the Hawkesbury

(ringing Brooklyn) up into the blue-tempered
mountains, away at Cessnock and Singleton district

along the Shoalhaven—a flame stampede in
bandit outbreaks,
                rearing at suburban backyards

of Glenorie, Berowra Heights, Galston,
                finally holding off at Arcadia.

Phaethon would have continued on his
careering journey had not Jove,
                indomitable and insulted,

blasted out his lightning bolt
                to shatter both boy and chariot—

pledge of fatherhood that destroyed Phaethon, broken.

When summer mismanages heat the same scenario
is played out time and again, whole forests then buckle in

ruin before flame and cinder.

THE GOD PARTICLE

Moon built, soft fires within cloud gorges.
Sun flares make burning mermaids whose solar winds
cry out centrifugally to buffet the earth,

knock out satellite transmissions, stall lifts,
blow a candlelit city into blackness, double birth rates.

Is the breath blown redly into clay, adamic.

Is presence in hurried retreat to creation's singularity.

Is thought-shock in waves billowing through space.

For this God it must mean that the future seen
                    is rejection
whose slow apology unrolls into destruction—

so it is we carry the sins of the father,
                    our backs bent as this globe over
to please as we backflip into disaster

through every ideal played, every invention made,
pulling at the innards of the earth

until we pull from its core the red fire to bathe in
hatred and love, interchangeable,
                    one searing pain for another exchanged.

See God's cheeks bloat and fill with fiery spittle
peering above dawn's horizon
                    clouds blown to the Four Corners.

Whose love cannot let go a creation that mocks creation.
Imperfection from perfection made?
                    Good day! The joke falls hard upon us.

THE DESERT AS PALIMPSEST

'St. Elmo's fire', '*Fata Morgana*', 'will-o'-the-wisp',
'Castor and Pollux', '*ignis fatuus*', 'corposant',

                  corpus sanctum, the sacred body made
desecrate;
              the pale and foolish fire
blown thin over bombed out craters and rubble:

pink-mist (pink mist) [*US military slang*] *n.*

A human body vaporized by 'bunker-busting'
bombs that leave only a pink-mist as sole evidence

of human remains; a term first used by the US military
during the Afghanistan war in 2002.

             Over the pottery coloured deserts,
a pattern of stars wraps around the earthly vessel.

The Tigris River unwinds its bloody bandage at sunrise
through Baghdad, small arms fire mingles with
             the muezzin call to the hour of prayer.

River mist or tank fire blurs the stately date palms.

Baghdad is a display case, smashed, memory wiped;
in the Iraq National Museum, the night filled corridors

reek oil-lit rags and the condensation of fear beading
the foreheads of the iconoclasts

                            / the swarming rabble
looting the underground vaults
plundering Sumerian and Babylonian artefacts

from 5000 BCE, stone bulls,

cuneiform tablets, ivory figurines, Nubian statuettes,
ceramic jars and urns—

Nineveh in fragments, Mesopotamia in ruins,

the City of Ur laid waste of its treasures in a city
cross-hatched by tank tracks—back to an engraved

granite-quartz block, next to the trimmed hedge,
                    under the playing fountain
fronting Liberty Enterprises guided by the principle:

'war is the pressure valve of techno-determinism'.

Rashid the Pavement Artist
                    squats in the ruined market place
and makes a mosaic out of metal fragment

and glass shards—depicts scenes of Baghdad;

donkeys made of brick bits, Euphrates/Tigris rivers,
animal rib bone curving back as scimitars

                        across a desert of potsherd:
life made frantic by the freedom anger engenders.

Let tribal memory float unperturbed upon
these two rivers where the sun places its golden harp.

Averroes holds in one hand 'intellect' in the other 'faith';
may peace descend upon the desecration of this city.

Can the sandstorms erase the hanging question of
'double truth': is the shadow as real as the object that

casts it, does ignorance make of anger a religion,
are the lessons of destruction a philosophy to die by?

Bless this first land first witness to the Written Word.

UNMANNERLY WEATHER REPORTED

Sydney's late autumn rains pass,
in blue-grey patches; to blue distances, not violet.

A plane, visible by its noise, washes away.

The tiny, stitched lights of the oil refinery toward
                Botany Bay ignite dusk.

The Warragamba Dam drops back a further few feet to
water restriction levels—no rain back of Bowral
                or Mittagong.

Night lowers fugitive as a water table.

Cyclone Barry fidgets over the Indian Ocean,
gnaws indolently along the West Coast to Port Hedland.

Like a wisdom that comes with loss
                that might even be expectation

the Morning Glory arrives off Burketown out of
                the Gulf of Carpentaria,
a rolling, unbroken cloudbank, 1,000 kilometers long.

Morning Star cresting
                the cloudy wave frozen in its fall.

One fishing boat hovers over
The Deep Western Boundary Current, visible by its

inch long, white tufted wake
            chasing a bloom of plankton.

OUT OF SHADOW INTO FIRE

I camp under the shadow of my brow,
and make marks upon the curved, inner wall of
                    my cranium.

Memory of lights come in waves,
the question is one of darkness and vacuum.

Shapes reflex, recoil and spread,
recalling muscle movement then the birth of fear.

Once someone who was me left his village
and his language behind him,

                    changed his country and diet

stood up only to look back,
froze at the sight—hurried forward, grew tall,

walked and camped for thousands of years;
who had learnt to look over his shoulder.

Rendered information back into symbol, image,
a sacrifice shaping flame in ochre and charcoal.

A hush, 'the bowstring's music',
                    then dead silence—the gods
who fell mortals themselves long fallen.

Struck down by the machine's godless hum.

Many gods make tributaries of memory,
while one god does of memory an absence make;

splitting infinity with the feathered shaft
of logic deducted back through the planetary spheres,

whose crystalline music first seen geometrically
in the marble temples
                    on hillsides themselves

glimpsed from afar as galaxies upholding space,
bright altars for the dry crackling of stars on blackness.

Death enters you as thought—its exit wound is vision.

FOR NIGHT TO ROLL ITS CAMBER OVER

The ruddy glare,
                    yellow, blurs its palette in rain,
at the boundaries of vision

flaring to white, blindingly, passes on (reassuringly)
                    into darkness, a rubbery hiss.

August is the windiest month,
west, sou'westerlies rattle the Sydney basin.

Light beams search down through underside
of cloud where planes lower unwaveringly toward

                    North East, South West runways.

A machine screams slowly backwards over rooftops
(a sound that moves away-and-toward)

pushing space apart, seemingly swallowing itself.

Reverberations directly overhead wrap around
the room you're in and rooming under

                    for night to roll its camber over.

TRICKS OF THEORY ALIGHT

Love by association
                is remembering that I
lost you completely to a land we once inhabited.

As if some time far back a misread
direction found us together in the same place.

As to who arrived first became
                in our turn an argument at departure.

We both got what we deserved, some part
of each other, something lost, or never given back.

Turning down off that sheer plateau,

the journey advanced into dusk—this resembled
dawn as a fossil, unearthed.

Remembering then, we looked up, found nothing
there left to recall.
                An echo we had walked away from.

Call out to the book laden poet,
'How many words does it take to sound nothing?'

MINISTRATIONS AT MIDNIGHT

Thunder remembered from an hour ago.

Silently like spilt milk the last of the lightning
slips back off the late night sky, a darkening smear that
                    slews to the south.

My Greek neighbour is hosing down her concrete
backyard in a time of water restrictions.

I can't see her, but hear the cooling hiss of water
hollowing out the humidity.

The planes overhead have ceased,
                    except for an intermittent, small craft
dimly buzzing in from some country district—

heading toward the Argus-eyed,
                    light industry of Botany Bay.

Between me and it,
a few bats click over terra-cotta angled rooftops ...

Metempsychosis pushes memory through
                    the lower order of genes, nothing relayed,
and nothing received.

While a thought like a moth drops below radar.

Harrington Street, Enmore, January 22, 2004

THE GREAT THIRST

The Murray River is more gecko than river.

Mud sticks—they say,
but in this case, it's the river that sticks to mud;
pinned under the tines of dead gum trees.

Sludging along river banks,
a river clot within its artery pushing
to empty into the sea, but doesn't, not quite.

The river mouth chocked up with sand
goes débouché, débouché, goes cough, cough,
no good to man nor beast.

The Murray River is more gecko than river.

Sucked dry by cotton irrigation,
stripped raw by chemical pollutants.

Oh, the way it lies, flat on its back, gasping;
suddenly you see river's lost its way—
backward looking, you might say.

Soon the red carpet of a desert will roll river up
and chuck what remains over its shoulder.

Maybe someone will discover
that discarded, rolled-up carpet
thrown into some dirty corner, some day?

The Murray River is more gecko than river.

IT'S RAINING

after Eugenio Montale

It's raining
                on the lone silky oak
behind the old guest house
                in Harrington Street, Enmore.

It's raining
                on the *trompe l'oeil* in
passing diesel exhaust of an overpass at sunset
amidst grey-blue plumes.

It's raining
                on the dead pot plant of
an indeterminate species on the rusty fire escape
by the windowsill
                with the filthy curtain.

It's raining barbarously
                on the rail crossing at
Blackheath and on the Hydro Majestic Hotel
overlooking Megalong Valley.

                It's filling up silences
and soaking the beer coasters.

It's raining piteously
                on the eyelashes of transvestites
up Oxford Street, it's raining at taxi ranks
and on real estate hoardings
                all over the city.

It's raining because youth
               is a programme about
limitless distances and romantic cul-de-sacs
and is, thankfully, blind to it.

It's raining on the grave
               of my father in Kelburn,
Wellington (which I've never visited) and it's raining
on my mother's
               grave next to his.

It's raining on Brooklyn Hills,
               on the clay, root-bound paths
that weave throughout Central Park,

on the tin roof of the weatherboard bach
by the hissing gas jet,

               on a windy night
up valley and hill *owt-the-back* of Karepa Street.

It's raining on Melbourne,
               on another design concept
made to reassure the citizens

of that city that God-given urbacity
               will protect them forever
within a Florentine fantasy.

It's raining on the spiral staircase of
                the double helix as genetics weighs
mortality against moral aesthetics
                in the interests of productivity.

It's raining on dismantled byways
                on voyages and faded memory.

On Naxos,
                island of marble and pine grove,
island of blue retsina and poppy *luminiferous*.

SNOW SCRIPT

A flock apart that breaks formation
                completes the sky's escutcheon.

An old timber church stands sketched in snow.

                A couple of trees with branches
crossed tight as seat belts.

Icy-pearled fishing boats in the bay.

An Icelandic movie set in the 18th century,
                an isolated fishing community.

The lone cry of the sea dove above the hill behind.

A villain, a severe winter, a little boy
                and survival which is all about death.

Coldness brings out the bully in the pastor
                gripping his pulpit like a dog sled.

The dogs out in the whiteness
expectant or bored bark at nothing much.

                The dogs go this way and that,
bunch down in the weather.
                A storm's coming but that's nothing new.

Just how bad keeps the community ruminating
over recriminations and small, warm hatreds.

The director's notes uncovered in the ruins
indicate a chase, one escape, and a large accident.

AN IMPERIAL CHRIST OF THE DUNES

'To have news value is to have a
                    tin can tied to one's tail,'
said T.E. Lawrence.

Booofh! sans-djinn;
up goes another supply train in a swirl of sand.

Soon enough, the Turks put a price on your head,
that amused you—tickled your pals back at HQ.

The race was on to reach Damascus
                    heart of the Arab people

before the British could get there for the imperial
carve up in a dirty deal done with the French.

To see into the future is to risk prophecy—see?
Though the game is the same the game is up:

is God a cigarette lighter?
is God a candy bar or pak of gum?
is God a coke bottle?

You and your small expeditionary force floated
                    about the desert like 'a thing intangible'.

Sorties made and victories gained—you became fame.

Later, unsettled, caught between two worlds,
a dreadful nostalgia claimed you.

You found escape through speed,
             floundering in a country lane.

SHELTON LEA, OTHER SIDE OF THE YARRA

IM: S.L. died, Friday 13, May 2005

            You were the last to see me off
out of Melbourne in '95, my two-year sojourn come of a close;

called by in a friend's BMW, your troubled limp taking you

halfway up the drive way to my apartment in
                Kelvin Grove, Armadale,
on the 'wrong side of the Yarra' for you. Calling out my name,
                impatiently—

to take me for a farewell drink
                (where others had turned their backs)
to your quiet watering hole in Ivanhoe.

                You played the pokies, I smoked your cigarettes,
we drank, easy in each other's company;

the world's concerns, of small concern, to us then.
                A quiet afternoon's camaraderie.

That gesture of kindness / recognition I have not forgotten.

You were, of course, a born performer,
your grainy, sandstone voice delivered your poems with an
                Old World charm.

Shelton, you are now well and truly the other side of the Yarra—
waved off, I am sure, by many of the ghosts you, in turn, saluted.

I see you heading out over grey plains, a knapsack full of lyrics,
                    away to your own country,
slowly turning to see streetlights come on over Clifton Hill.

CHARLES HAMILTON SORLEY

WWI poet, killed in the Battle of Loos, 13th October, 1915, age 20

Long before a sniper's bullet to the head,
          witherward over the Marlborough Downs
in rain and wind you found your god.

At one with the 'millions of the mouthless dead' your songs and
dreams live on in Sorley's Weather.

Capt. R. Graves claimed you as 'one of the three poets of
          importance killed during the war'

along with Rosenberg and Owen (no mention of Brooke).
          You sought it seemed a 'practical' poetry

devoid of sentiment, stripped bare of self, hands reaching
          down into earth.

A windblown hill pleased you; what was elemental,
ghosts in pale battalions passing, grey, billowing days,
          the bitter rain.

Aoidos of raw and windy weather,
          over the downs your ghost runs past
'Where the old battered signpost stands'.

'Sorley's Weather'. A poem by Robert Graves (1895-1985)
in Fairies and Fusiliers. 1918.

Of the Greek, aoidos; reciter or singer of Homeric poetry;
rhapsode, minstrel. The term is used in C.H.S's poem: 'To J.B'.

OF BLUE INTO WHITENESS

1.

Distant as an altar chime
                    thinly flung over Enmore, the single
Sunday bell knocks soft.

                    Such extravagance in
its pale sounding, muted consonants, which in half rhymes

                    heard high off brick walls or window panes
from a near-distant slate roof

that boasts its belfry—*there*,
                    as morning crowds out small minutes
imbricated on the hour.

                    Climate decides reverie and heat diffuses it;
can one become immune to revelation?

In the outer chambers beyond the earth's rub
                    the Hubble telescope
extracts another buffed, opalescent galaxy.

The feathered image strikes home its pixelated prayer.

2.

Black-winged, grackle of thunder,
                    (out of our dreams we materialize into light)
a work crew of earliest gods banging

away at the world's foundations.

Building against the mystery of nothingness
                    against the ache found in absence;

an endless disappearance of blue into whiteness,
                    and then black, solid as unbelief

all through the hours of our days
into the chronological beat of mortal hearts.

                    When the fabled toyshop came alive at night
did it imagine itself a SFX department a century hence?

The sixth sense is nothing other than heightened
                    awareness of what is going on—now.

Who fears second sight has everything to hide.

3.

That which is capable of being seen will ever
                exist beyond our capability for seeing it.

Too much matter inhabiting too much
                'nothingness'.

We live in suspense, and duly, are suspended.
                'Welcome home, traveller!'

From sleep to wake did you in your passing
leave a past come back to haunt you long after life had left?

How much you missed in your vigilance;
                from sculptor to poet, forging

the missing link until that which came after came first.

Turn this way—address the tribunal—
                for soon you will awake to your calling.

PRAYER, NIGHT MANOEUVRES

A night of buffeting, big winds
                    at close combat with the city, the flower
tub on my balcony remains steady, anchored.

                    A solid night's sleep
as darkness, making its presence felt, insists that
the mind folds low to its burrow.

                    We create in the mind's eye by aeons
simulacrum and cumulative fear;
                    from the cave to the nave.

A thing so monstrously refulgent
                    as though all our days never existed
that allows us to exist yet.

                    O troubled and beauteous lie

take my praise, remind me to look left/right before
I cross, curse myself, accurse others against vulnerability.

                    Condemn me to doubt,
I implore, let me hear the soul yawn, sleeplessly,
                    within its damaged temple.

Harrington Street, Enmore, March 25, 2005

THIS HIDDEN FRONTIER

1.

Grapevine tangling the camphor laurel,
                wattle, garden shed, indeterminate growth as
understory, whose leaves bruise into autumn.

Clouds lead elsewhere, continuously distant,
                out toward the flattening, long light.

A section of Kingsford Airport set between
                roof gables pools the last of the afternoon sun.

Suburban trains curving, bend acoustically, out of sight,
rummage amongst floorboards, joists, nor'east facing structures.

All along this hidden frontier,
                rivets click on sleepers, under wheels.

Daymoon as watermark.
Buried behind a chimney stack. Ghost, hung on a roof aerial.
                At flight.

Movement governed by shadow,
and shadow the recognition of it; later, a moon-cauled headlight.

An Indian summer eats into the cooler months;
                through slow days,

the old Greek next door, removes bits of twig and stem,
drops the purple clusters into a large plastic pithos, then seals it.

A week later, he sets
an iron hand press over a grey, wooden cask to crush the grape,
and release a shadowy, purple stream, the colour of storm.

2.

Morning become a black and white documentary;
                brass band of the Salvation Army fading in

and out of the hour on the breeze,
(old imperialist sentiments) tuba pumping the 'Word of God'

                from a not too distant park, this Sunday.

I think of the Vauxhall Velox, Morris Oxford, Zodiac,
                Humber Hawk and Austin 60,
under a few stippled clouds that flatten like kipper on a plate.

3.

Shadow props up autumn light glaze,
                stacks cloud stadium 360 degrees.

In the Southern Highlands, Goulburn washes itself in a plastic
bucket, its Pejar Dam water level below 12 percent and falling.

Townships high and dry.

Water tankers slowly sidle down country roads, cattle in
pens stand rib-to-rib, the 'Big Dry'

                    grips the mind of the suicide.

Here in Enmore, ethnic custom remains intact;
the old Greek lady next door (perennially) in her blue smock
                    washes, soaps and hoses

her son's Dairy Farmers truck once a week, top to bottom,
doing her bit to drain the Warragamba Dam.
                    All night, every night, her son glued

to cable TV, eyes irradiated under the pulse
of colour from the living room, a Punch & Judy light show

flares and flickers behind lacy curtains,
as though all the world's wars had come home to visit;

                    plushly silent up and down the spectrum.

Should it sometime rain about these parts, she will
redouble her efforts, hosing down a small concrete backyard,
                    to rid herself of the run off.

4.

Loneliness, welcome. You seek distance, always;
                    and there, green—no, one emerald light,

between black night clumps (stilled tree crowns)
                    in the pitch of the hour.

No horizon, though this may, in part, pass for that

                    'dislocated place'.

Night signals its triumph, once more,
                    and the eye focuses the perfect blur.

Above cities stars disrupt stellar intersections
                    made newly reverberant by this darkness.

(Is) velvet whisper, unheard, that fathers forth all thought
                    toward one emerald light, chemical, and soulless.

SHOULD ANGELS DANCE ON A PINHEAD

O the perfect firework!
Immaterial, an endless exposition in celebration of
itself, unto itself, toward?

Ergo: that which exists, exists in order
to celebrate its own existence: ergo: beauty that
lies within those ordered, serried ranks.

Though, the devil's in the detail,
slyly, questioning the admission of any existence by
admitting to it, faultlessly.

Sky italicized by light streak an
event foretold to break thought barrier.

For ten weeks, a convocation of professors
argued the toss and quizzed the proposition,
mercilessly:

'the infinitely subtle problem of
the Imaginary Object vibrating out

in empty space, and whether it can be fed off
Secondary Intentions.'

Thus debated at the 'Council of Constance'
in Rabelais' Gargantua and Pantagruel.

Such fancy footwork by a million angels
                    occupying no particular space or
one devil, maybe, hands in pockets,

          spinning on a dime

would exponentially enthral a Legation of Language Poets
          chimaera bombinans in vacuo
                              regardless.

OUTING THE ORDINARY

        Middle American barn style,
its roof spade-angled sharply to guttering, unseemly,
light orange terra-cotta roof tiles.

        Plastic tongue & groove,
two bright green cypress trees, sentinels, offsetting
frontage and portico, one a whisper

        taller than the other . . .

In this once behind and back down neighbourhood
                the move against
a tussle of Greek families holding still to the old

working class terraces, one part wrapped in grapevine,
                the other bougainvillea

up against the chic colour tones of neo-economic
migrants from the northern suburbs, mobile and uppity,
                making a fist of it.

A handful of handkerchief sized parks by concrete
                culverts, flights of scatterbrain pigeons, the
ubiquitous sparrow not seen these parts.

        Fair play of weather,
equal opportunity of daylight, disgruntled gardens
                full of miniature gnomes

affront hydrangeas under low windowsills—
                    the old and the new and older still,
night sky arranged into corridors, landing strips dimly lit;

(stars pack the sides of sky full as a warehouse)
                    for all unseen arrivals & departures

from this earth that makes its offerings regardless of our
                    entreaties to and from and by,
amongst platoons of suburbs, shoulder to shoulder,

                    between second hand car lots,
one after the other, restacked every 5 km or so by an IGA
                    or Coles Supermarket.

                    A wintry, star-stunned sky
in febrile clusters, old warrior campfires signalling that nothing
                    ever goes away

or if it does, is always arriving, and is pre-programmed.

MAROONED

Groups of gulls at intervals
heading to the mountain, and the sea
                the other side of it;

to a stretch of blue-grey water in a
                gully reservoir, or a refuse tip.

Dead tree spars folding through—
                a grey quilt over its flanks.

The 'organ pipes' (dolerite columns)
                hang from the summit
as though baleen in the mouth of a whale.

I have looked on the mountain
for six days now and yet cannot move it.

As we are inhabited by our (owned)
imaginations too greater weight upon the word

reduces that world to rubble
                strewn beneath the sun's revolution,
or caught in the moon's titanium glare.

Cascade Road / South Hobart. January 7, 2006

LONE SHUNTER

The lit, landed dish that is Te Kuiti
                back flips momentarily before my eyes

into the bowl-like configuration of
                Wellington harbour—those running lights,

yellow along Old Petone Road; Rimutakas
                nothing yet where that bulk blackness holds.

Here, the 'lone shunter' wolfs through
                the centre of town
flashing flamenco signal lights the last wagon behind.

                In a small, Eastern European enclave
a laden cart over cobblestone
                presupposes thunder.

I am here, a Trotsky in Te Kuiti,
                the first time a black sky seen in years.

The Milky Way adrift, as smoke from
some distant campfire; krill-like, a god's wet dream.

There are women who press upon your breath
                like master organ players, to make or break.

I am here, isolate,
Te Kuiti. Omphalos. Limestone country.
These hills that dip and trough could

leave you swamped, the sky a swagger.

Harrier Hawk switches to remote half way between paddock
and halfway house, spiralling, radial, ever reliable stage prop.

Wind that tumbles north through trees
bringing the sound of rushing water over troubled contours.

As if in that stillness from the night before
the morepork had orchestrated this hour.

I am here, overseeing morning fog,
twenty years shunted to a siding the other side of the Tasman.
That city. *That bullwhip.* Sydney.

INTERCOLONIAL

'*And the sea breathes brine*
From its strange straight line'
　　—Thomas Hardy

Tusked cauliflowers and herded carrots, onions in piles,
tumbled pumpkins, potato scree, boxed and stalled in between
scales that swung and creaked from the cream cabin roof
of the Indian greengrocer's Bedford truck, his weekly

round by the winding way of Helen and Apuka streets,
right to the hill top ridge and Brooklyn-*west*; our feudal hearth
in Karepa Street, perched high over the Wellington basin,
that bounced off hill quakes about *Te Whanga-nui-a-Tara*.

Nightly, the harbour dilated pupil-bright; the Rimutaka Range
encircled, drew closer; a lamp black border torn from the sky hem;
the two islands, Somes (Matiu) and the smaller, Ward Island
(Mākaro) slowly contracted, sank from view; navigational lights

blinked one to the other and back again, in the throat of
Tory Channel, unhurriedly; the city rose like some luminescent
fish caught, hung up there in a net of stars, spilling light;
or dyed the clouds dirty orange that coiled diagonally south.

Our bay windows became a ship's bridge, took the full force
of southerlies off the Tasman Sea, churned smoky-grey as
charcoal on wintry nights, the house held to its moorings against
shuddering troughs, deep low-pressure systems; the fireplace

in the lounge roaring on through the pitching dark, city
lights below shattered into a million raindrops smeared across
the windowpanes, electrical as phosphorescence breaking
on the crest of a wave, as the squall hit hard, again and again.

The macrocarpa tree overhanging the bach, thickset as
a nightclub bouncer, buckled and straight in its lean all at once;
one palm spread protectively, waving the bach back, while
yet twisted to face away, toward the stucco family house.

Its guardianship grew outside my bedroom window as
though declaring on a windy night, this was the correct distance
that must be kept between the two buildings, the stucco
homestead, and the squat weatherboard bach, as if stating—

the bach would once again serve as original sanctuary;
gas wall-heater hissing quietly with its yellow and orange flame.
The air warm through long dark months—that became my
safe house, away from the main house, serious as a fortress.

Before the great fire break at the bottom of our street
(the short end) its yellow gash bulldozed wide as any highway
dove down to Aro Street; before the roaring pine grove
that became our 'Sherwood Forest', hard by the turnaround,

its floor ankle deep in copper needles, fell to the chainsaw;
before the *Wahine* storm tore up the pine belt along the farther,
westernmost ridge above Karori reservoir *out-the-back*
of our place; before Mt Victoria got scalped by a summit road.

Rimutaka ridges snowcapped. Fog rolling off harbour hills.
Framed by our casement windows—a time of trolleys, flax slides,
and tumbledown forts, of toetoe brandished as war plumes,
hidden footpaths and short cuts, and WWII concrete bunkers.

When the council-red, No. 7 Brooklyn-*west* bus wearily
wound its way, around Karepa Street (the long end) skirting by
'forbidden' *Fitchett's Farm*, winding down precipitous
Todman Street, to the Brooklyn village of my childhood below.

This boyhood harbour town for an oracular voice strung
out over fracture and fault, whose bass notes foretold the story,
the *Wellington Fault*, first of those major breaks, emerges
west of Sinclair Head, running through the packed hills back

of Karori suburb, and under the main reservoir, out across
Brooklyn-*west*, down through Thorndon by the entrance to the
bottleneck, under Radio ZLW, the telegraph station on
top of Tinakori Hill, out along the marine terraces to Petone by

the Heretaunga Valley basin, tremulations under the reclaimed
land of the inner city, transmissions down the capital's
spine (seismic rumour) the hum at the back of the head of every
Wellingtonian—deep seated bass notes sounded through the

Ohariu Fault that extends west of Tongue Point into Porirua
Basin, by the *Black Swans of Pāuatahanui*, by the floating
gables of the Old Manse, by Brady's Grave and Duck Creek,
riding up against the mud flats and Paekākāriki foothills.

In the Upper Hutt Valley the *Akatarawa Fault* cuts
northwest 18 kilometers off the *Wellington Fault* to merge
with the Moonshine and Otaki Forks Fault system each
anchored in a tug-of-war to the Pacific and Australian plates.

The *Wairarapa Fault* crash tackled Wellington Harbour—
pushed up wide tracts of waterfront property in the
1855 quake (2000-year return time). Shoulders sideways to
strike north. Dives under the Tararua–Rimutaka ranges.

The low lying *Pukerua Fault* journeys from Oterongo
to Pukerua Bay, like a lone shark patrols the shallow waters
between these two points; the last, most elusive note,
the *Wairau Fault*, serpentine, solitary, forks off the Alpine,

coils out across Cook Strait, through submerged canyons,
banks and plateaux, sea valleys, troughs and table mounts;
raddled cables of energy (revived or recalled) through
a childhood that cartwheeled like the blades of a windmill.

A.D. 1460. Hao-whenua, 'earth-wrecker' hard riding that
quake breakneck through the Holocene and post-glacial ages,
7000 years in his wake, the Wairarapa and Wellington
fault lines wrapped round his wrists, tight as bush lawyer,

pulling first at one, then the other, lifting basement blocks
in a grand tilt under the Great Harbour of Tara; that horseshoe-
shaped island, *Motu-kairangi*, shudderingly, become peninsula;
the throat of the channel, *Te Awa-a-Taia*, choked with rock.

Wellington Harbour, hill-ringed, rumoured as landlocked,
the lake home of taniwha—*Ngake*, held fast in a fault line net,
shook loose to force passageway into Cook Strait,
leaving in its turbulent wake, *Te Au-a-Tane*, entrance through

to *Te Whanga-nui-a-Tara*—its outline shaped like that of
the colossal squid, millennia before Kupe chased the 'sea cloud'
of an octopus leagues across the Great Ocean of Kiwa,
caught and killed it off *The Brothers* rocks in *tapu* Raukawa.

When the city dissolves to a ghost, drizzled through the
moonless night of Happy Valley, the Ōwhiro Stream advances
from the eastern slopes of the Te Kopahou ridge to
the western side of the Tawatawa hills, stretching its black

ribbon toward Ōwhiro Bay on the south coast, strewn with
the busted boilers of iron barques, ribs and hulls of
full-rigged, wooden ships and schooners; *Cyrus*, the *Progress*,
Helios, *Woollahra*, sea litter spread from Cape Terawhiti

to the 'Siren Rocks', snagged and snared in the teeth of the
Roaring Forties on *Toka-haere* (Thoms Rock) off Tongue Point;
a 'demon rock' where the greater number of ships foundered
on the mile long reef—a rock it's said that had the power

to shape-shift in a fog bandaged hour, yet it was the full
flood tides and thumping gales on that coast claimed most lives,
and left as sea wrack—*St. Vincent, City of Dunedin, Halcione,*
the *Grasmere, Nambucca, Willie McLaren, SS Penguin . . . .*

6: PM, February 12, 1909. The steamer departed Picton,
sea with barely a tilt to it, night sky polished as glass, the weather
started out fine with a light swell, then closed in half way
across the straits, turned beast upon reaching Tory Channel.

Horns ploughed mountainous waves, bellowed a raging
southerly—the Minotaur seeking its labyrinth, massive head
rolling this way and that, frantic, as the horizon twanged,
then broke and dropped out of sight—only the breath of the

beast could be heard foaming in the waves. Captain Naylor
decided on an outside course against 'a big southerly set',
sought Pencarrow light, but that lay cloaked under thick fog.
The SS *Penguin* struck Thoms Rock starboard side 10: PM,

a mile and a quarter off Cape Terawhiti—'water making
fast the chain locker and fore cabins'—of the two boats swung
out, one smashed against the ship's hull, women and children
tossed upon the turbulence, the other swamped, soon capsized.

Of the 105 aboard, 75 drowned, 30 got ashore. Parting from
her husband, 'Cheer up, old man,' Ada Hannam called, 'Goodbye,'
came the reply. Tackle gave way, the lifeboat pitched head
first, her four children drowned, she the only woman to survive.

A cold slug of ocean water flooded the engine room—hit
the red-hot boilers that exploded like depth charges inside the belly
of the ship (she segmented long before the explosion faded)
went down bow first, a few leapt off the stern into blackness.

Bodies floated face down on the floodtide, stared sightlessly,
for something wrenched from the grasp; taffrail, child or an adult's
hand—and barrel rolled over, as though into another dream—
drifted away from the SS *Penguin* strewn across the sea floor.

The column of the drowned listed in the *Colonist*, February
15, 1909, stood tall as a mast; passengers and crew both:
the chief steward and the trimmer, saloon waiter and the second
officer, fireman and boatswain, donkeyman and able seaman,

the third officer and the scullion, the greaser and the chief
engineer; every passenger on the SS *Penguin* caught between
home and employment: cable maker and steel worker,
railway station manager, stock inspector, boot factory man,

crockery merchant, flax dresser and student; wives, maids,
and mothers tumbled along an eight mile stretch of coast between
Cape Terawhiti and Sinclair Head; bodies, kelp and wreckage,
one upturned lifeboat hull gleaming white as a whale's belly.

From the eastern reaches of the Hutt Valley plain by
sweeping bends and forested hills, the broad, slow flowing
Wai-whetu Stream eased to the Te-Awa-Kairangi estuary
(sandy flat and flax marsh) at Petone beach—a waterway

navigable by small schooners for two miles upstream
as far as *Wilcox's Shipyard & Mill*—before the 1855 earthquake
lifted the foreshore—the Wai-whetu, netting the Milky Way,
'starry stream', 'star stream', and the creak of canvas.

A few yet remain, as palimpsest, overlaid by the
harbour city, lines drawn upon water damaged parchment
(colour of clay, forests clear-felled) of the original
town planner's blueprint; streams, or tracery of streams.

The Whakahikuwai Stream falling from the eastern slopes
of Tinakori ridge, swirls through Hobson and Murphy streets,
to enter the ferny, deep ravine of Hobson Street gully,
spreading out across the lost flatlands of Haukawakawa

(Thorndon Terrace) from the southern end of Molesworth
Street the earthbound mirrors of the Wai-titi Stream slide past
the *Hotel Cecil*, lifting the sandy beach at Bowen Street
in a burst of light; the Wai-tangi in a gentle fan of water rises

from beneath the Wellington Hospital grounds to join
the small, whispering streams of Mt Victoria, gathering
sluggishly to push through Newtown, and through the lower
reaches of Adelaide Road, to the Basin Reserve, turning

into Cambridge and Kent Terraces, its waters beaching
at Courtenay Place; here the waiting lagoon breaks into peat,
flax-rooted islets that float out across the harbour; the Wai-papa
Stream rises from the south eastern slope of Mt Victoria,

through the gully at the north end of Alexandra Road, past
the Hataitai tram tunnel, to meet the sister branch at Arawa Road;
together—they flow between Hataitai, Waipapa roads,
rustling through Ruahine Street and Moxham Avenue to escape

down the Kilbirnie Crescent incline; from the slopes of
Puke-hinau ridge, the Wai-koukou Stream gathers into a pool
on the corner of Willis and Manners streets, *where the forest birds
come to bath*, to join the harbour at lower Boulcott Street.

The Tutae-nui Stream laves through the old Church of
England cemetery on the north side of Bolton Street, reaches
Bowen Street, and there curves round the Cenotaph to
Lambton Quay's original shoreline; the Pipitea Stream rises

below Raroa Road, flows past the Karori traffic tunnel,
down Tinakori Road to Hawkstone Street, fanning out across
the Haukawakawa flatlands, under the Te Rae-kai-hau,
cliff-salient, *'headland that eats the wind'*; into the harbour.

From Polhill's Gully the Wai-mapihi crosses flatlands,
skirting the *Royal Oak Hotel* east of Cuba, south of Manners
streets, to beach there. Again, the Miramar Peninsula
breaks from the mainland to become Motu-kairangi island—

at its centre (a great red lake) the low-lying *Vale of Para*.
Hear the harbour breathe; ghosts of the spring fed Awa-mutu,
Kumutoto, Wai-paekaka, Tiaki-wai, the Korokoro, Te Poti,
gone to ground (creek and stream) in a babble of tongues.

Mt Victoria, its crown circumcised by a ring road.
Mt Victoria, scalped with a yellow gash around its summit.
Mt Victoria, home to the taniwha that turned into a bird.
Tangi te keo, the wailing of wind and bird screech.

'**O**ur lank shadows dogging us, scrambling across the
raw-red stones', cried the explorers, the oven plate of Central
Australia; the Gibson and Simpson and Great Sandy deserts;
each shadow elongated into history like a Drysdale painting.

What they believed in was the Inland Sea, something
wholly cool and soft, habitable heat became the one thing
they held in common, heart of the continent a drinkable well.
Destiny ungovernable? Through us to earth's iron heart,

our faces as mirrors upturned to all that the universe pours
through them; painless, dead silent, to find an involuntary
response *neutrinoed* by values not of our making; pain
endlessly arced via rainbow voltage, from behind the sun's

solar wind, its molten worm mass, or come by galaxies'
runic configurations; diamond tipped, churned through sidereal
time and space: *what we look like back from what we look at.*
O innumerable quandaries asked of light and legacies made.

Spindrift, a curtain rising upon the biscuit-based sea cliffs
and the clacking gulls, that mix thickly with the brush stroked,
grey-blue waters (a memory of sail and steam) to announce a
friable continent, iron filings gathered redly about its red

heart, the night sky engrained black under an ashen moon.
That yearning where gravity swoons off balance, the cypress
tree beside a sandstone wall, wistfully (remembered)
unstartles the senses to suggest other years—other departures:

baffle of winds at mid-harbour barbered the funnel smoke,
combed out black-backed gulls to the finer points of
sky around Port Phillip Bay and the steamer, SS *Ringarooma.*
Dublin born of the Irish diaspora, and 26 years resident

in Melbourne, he departed the looming depression to try
his hand further south, under the dough shaped harbour hills
of Dunedin: great-grandfather, Thomas McCormack,
sailed for Aotearoa in 1877, clouds in lit pews before him.

Behind him, Phillips, McWalter & Chambers foundry in
Carlton, Melbourne, where he learned his trade; behind him the
few weeks back in the '60s where he chanced his luck on
goldfields at Ballarat and Bendigo, but did not strike it lucky.

Behind him the brutality of the goldfield constables, ex-
convicts from Van Diemen's Land who on horseback rode
down Chinese miners, demanding evidence of licence,
the language not understood, and the beatings that followed.

McCormack witnessed one such beating and unseated the
constable from his horse, restrained, wrested the whip off him,
then horsewhipped the man in turn for his cruelty—escaped;
a warrant out for his arrest though no conviction recorded.

He would gain 'First Order of Merit' at the International
Exhibition, 1882, Christchurch, for his patent cooking range,
Zealandia, japanned black as a priest's cassock, brass
bars polished bright as candlesticks; his ornamental castings

for balconies, verandas, town railings gaining prize medals
in Melbourne and Dunedin exhibitions, his intricate iron grilles,
panels and gates gracing the entrance way and archways of St.
Joseph's Cathedral, finally dedicated (unfinished) in 1886.

A Catholic in a Calvinist/Scottish town (age: thirty six)
he planned a foundry. The Union Steam Ship Company's two
Intercolonial steamers, *Ringarooma* and *Arawata*, flyers both,
schooner-rigged, beating back waves on the Melbourne–Dunedin

line, winds westerly on the *transtasman* weekly mail run,
and he aboard the *Ringarooma* (Port Chalmers via Bass Strait)
though any given day must have offered packaged cloud,
roundly indecisive, while further out, clouds off the yards at

the foremast and Thomas McCormack on the hurricane deck
by the red funnel. An elsewhere-centred, colonial castaway
people on the wide awake sea breathed the business tides; they
came to construct (by the boatload) along with other far-

flung families where winds belted over waterfront clamour
that spoke of grabbed or gaffed chances had; only inland
was noticed the absence of village bell in the creaking
bush—unfamiliar; 1200 m. in the arc and loop of the Tasman

trade—its depths yet unsounded though rumoured—that
alive sound as sleet polished the dark, brightening the waves'
fenders, bending under her bronze green hull and hissing
between decks, coiling around derricks as the *Ringarooma*

slowed, heaved to 8 knots, her 1096 tonnage toiling luff by
bellicose headwinds, cutting up from Antarctica on the third day,
out across the Tasman Sea on this Wednesday crossing,
wave crescendo, elbowed by way of the Great Southern Ocean.

Like hurricane blasts (blue storms) off the very seabed itself,
common as salt here on this five day voyage by sou'east
latitudes. There is always a procession, contrawise,
the sperm and humpback whale, the right whale passing

over as if airborne over the Tasman Abyssal Plain,
the Cook Canyon and Chatham Rise, along the Kaikōura
Canyon down into the Kermadec Trench, the Milford Canyon,
the Aorangi Ridge and Akaroa Sea Valleys, the Kupe

Abyssal Plain and along the Lord Howe Seamount Chain
they sang, by way of the Cook Fracture Zone, high above Haast
Canyon, heading to polar waters, puzzled by the whine of
Compound Surface Condensing Engines (unanswerable) as they

headed along the Bligh Sea Valley over the Bounty Ridge
into a down draught current and on migratory paths;
by the Ross Sea and the Bay of Whales, riding shelf, shoal
and spur directed by the pilot light of blood and sea rhythm—

plots the memory's contours, the unwavering thought
of the mind's binnacle as McCormack thinks on the world with
all its bigness within reach, 'It is history makes it so,'
he says to no one, 'in or out of time,' as he heads back down

the companionway for the saloon set square amidships,
and in the lounge, to let his gaze fall upon mauve, Utrecht velvet
walls and walnut panelling, hiding him from the buckling
sea horizon in this weather sodden hour—now unlocatable.

McCormack recounts how, 'when quite a boy' in Hobart,
taking a coach to Launceston, on the morning of *Monday, 23rd*
July 1849, the passengers conversed amongst themselves,
ignoring 'A well-dressed, staid-looking man, of middle-age

and thoroughly respectable demeanour . . .' who sat beside
him, 'And in a very entertaining way, pointed out and described
whatever was interesting on the way,' north of Oatlands;
not once did he address the guard or passengers nor they him.

Quietly spoken and engaging, he made the long hours pass
pleasantly, the coach bumped along, stopping for dinner at Perth;
he alone stayed behind, and sat up on the coach roof to eat
his meal, while the others entered the hotel, 'to sit down at table'.

Ironbark logs roared and snapped in the wide, open fire place
as the hotelier remarked to the coach driver, 'Well, Phil, I see
you've got Solomon with you this trip.' And Phil replied,
'Yes, that cove in Launceston is to be turned off tomorrow,

he's a'goin' up to scrag him.' So the boy soon learned
who his travelling companion was, '*the notorious Solomon Blay,*
the common hangman'. When the coach set out once more,
McCormack 'took a fresh seat' for the final leg of the journey.

That Monday morning, walking by the *Red Lion Inn*,
the premises gave off a stagnant smell, as if exhausted from
the previous night's excesses, curtains the colour
of clotted blood hung limply in window frames—the reek

of whale oil lamps still thick upon the air, and out of
cobbled laneways, drifted an acrid stench of urine and rum;
everything there seemed cast in a gloomy light at this
early morning hour. As his coach ride to Launceston was not

due to depart Hobart Town for at least a couple of hours,
the boy headed on down to the docks, strolled along the quay,
toward the new wharf, refreshed by the chilly winds
gusting off the Southern Ocean. Mount Wellington loomed,

its crown laced with snow, mist in shreds, every now
and again, flurries of white powder scuffed up, yet as quickly,
settled back onto the mountainside, like the spume of
some leviathan, ' "organ pipes" (dolerite columns) hung from

its summit as though baleen in the mouth of a whale.'
A two-masted schooner hugged the wharf, canvas sail flapped
loosely in the encircling winds, as it gently rose and fell;
bold, blue lettering painted on the stern spelt out, *Lillias*.

He estimated that she weighed upwards of 90 ton—
a few windjammers tacked about the inner harbour, while
farther off, the bigger brigs and barques tugged at moorings,
as if impatient to weigh anchor and be on their way.

Already, barrels and bales had been offloaded, a horse
and two-wheeled cart waited wharfside. He looked out across
Sullivan's Cove to Battery Point, past ordnance stores,
to what he supposed must be the Harbour Master's house,

where just behind, at higher elevation, the old windmill
stood out sharply, its blades caught in the late morning light.
Mount Wellington seemed to him like some massive beast,
poised to slide into the harbour, and disappear out to sea.

McCormack, swung in the hammock of the sea, dreams.
'Wave roar'; an elevated, floating platform on four
giant, yellow towers. In diameter, greater than boles of giant
eucalypt or columns of Egyptian temples—latticework

of steel armatures—high enough for a ship to pass
safely under. A thousand lights clustered the black, rectangular
fortress. To McCormack, it appeared an industrial city,
massive and metalled as a wetback stove rose fifty stories

above waves, a yellow dragon flame plumed a gantry.
Cloud-hide pegged out at the corners horizoned—McCormack,
shipbound between the wind and tide (tossed by both)
in sleep that troubled deeply, across glacial moraine and rock

fall; to an Icelandic sunset—*holmgang* of cloud fastened in
hazelled lightning bolt. 'Blacksmiths forging iron, hurling molten
blocks onto the sea in the ship's wake,' he concluded.
Before him his forbear, *Cormac the Skald*, striding to contest;

yet his unforgiving lady, *Steingerd*, proved his undoing—
though in every heroic deed he upheld honour hard tested by
dawn raids over the Atlantic crests to Alba and Ireland—
where he fell, locked in mortal combat, against a giant Scot.

His face the colour of dead moonlight—under dark hair,
eyes black as stones. 'He lived before letters *destroyed the Art
of Memory*,' says McCormack, 'songs faithful as sea-tides—
his broadsword cried in battle, blood-wand reddened for booty.'

The Viking longboat drifts away on the tide as though
departing one dream and passing into another, solid as shadow,
silhouette. The boat is companion to half-light and the
afterlife—men ghosting the shoreline, indeterminate shapes.

Still as statues they watch. One column of flame rises up to
the stars from the burning pyre, a flawed sunset across
northern latitudes. The sea black, velvet. Light reflects dully off
iron shields. One by one the men turnabout and depart.

To the east, an island appeared, rotated in the wake of
the ship, at its centre, an iron compound with four watch towers;
behind barbed-wire fencing, a few bedraggled figures
hung in despair—all wore orange tunics and white skull caps,

all were chained at the wrists and feet, some gasped as
stranded fish, others (lips sewn shut) sat bowed, or kneeled.
At night, lanterns swung light beams into every corner;
shadowy jackals patrolled the *Island of the Asylum Seekers*.

In his ear all the while, continuous—the 'wave voice'
telling of blue storms, hinting at sea-clouds shadowing under
(Pelagian depths) soundings of the original sea with the
Ringarooma plying lat. 25°/50° South, long. 145°/180° East.

Echo sounding dream chambers bounce back and forth:
'Three things to guard against in sleep,' says McCormack,
'daring the mind leap off over the brink of an abyss,
kicking at imaginary ghosts, waking at the dead man's hour.'

He dreams: *Mundus Subterraneus:* from the earth's
molten core, caverns of fire and water, ocean and volcano,
through a network of underground channels feeding one
into another and circulating deep within the earth's interior.

He dreams a toxic dump widening in the pacific gyre,
a garbage patch the size of Abyssinia, bile ejected from the
gaping maw of some thrice-retching Charybdis, churned
bags and bottles, things broken small, opaque as nail clippings.

A place deprived of oxygen, an ocean desert devoid of
fish and fowl stretched far as eye could see, contagion shunned
by every sailor, for the dreck of the world accumulated here,
swept from the industrial wastelands of a brand new age.

A floating mass that seemed to reach out infinitely into
sea and sky, become indistinguishable, translucent as jellyfish,
an ocean heaving as 'marine lung' heavily lifted and slumped,
as McCormack in his ship's bunk rolled through the night.

He dreams a tornado, watery shaped, the ocean's navel,
obsidian black and sleek, funnelled, descending into the Pacific at
depth with an amplified roar like that of the ship's furnace;
the vessel itself twisting round and round the froth white collar.

A diorama of distorted, ghostly figures within his cabin
flitted on wall and ceiling, cast shadow nets over McCormack's
dreamscape, to capture past worlds or those yet to come,
while the bedside lamp glowed luminescent as the lanternfish.

The bach by the macrocarpa tree. A 1920s weatherboard,
rectangular structure. Pokey kitchen. One main room. Windows
facing north. Paint aged brown, cracked. Windowsills flaky,
brick red. Bargeboards book-ending the corrugated iron roof.

A young Hungarian woman rented the bach in those early
years (already resident when we took possession of the place).
Her little daughter's two plastic Barbie dolls, a luxury
the mother could barely afford, seemed preternaturally large;

the eyes clicked shut when you tilted them back, at least,
one eye did, the other fluttered half way closed, deathlike, that is
why I remember the Hungarian woman and her daughter,
rumoured to have fled her country to briefly seek sanctuary—

a disconsolate marriage from which she escaped, who lived
in the bach during the mid-'50s, I remember, because of the doll's
eyes, arctic blue and blind as marbles, also because my
brothers' affront forced her to flee again for the third time.

The bach set back against the Cassidys' high clay bank one
house removed up Karepa Street; the leaky gas stove, dangerous,
rarely used, the hissing gas jet of the wall heater, chalky
elements busted, miniature mediaeval battlements that glowed

yellow and orange as if forever catching some dying sunset,
the flame softly belly danced, susurrated warmth through the long
winter nights. One gargantuan oaken desk. One low chest
of books pushed up under the windowsill—abandoned dreams

of our father, contained all anyone ever wanted to know
about Russian Revolutions, founding fathers: Marx and Engels,
Lenin and Trotsky, tumbled into this mildewed, mass grave;
the bach I came to claim as my own, my sanctuary and retreat.

Lifting the lid, the musty odours, that chest of books under
the window, and what seemed to me impenetrable, dull
hardbacks, of men who stood before factory stacks, streaming
on a red sky, fists raised in salute, the hammer and sickle!

I crouched there under shadow of my pen that fell across
the barren white page, that lengthened solitary as a telegraph pole,
under the hiss of gas jet, shunted words back and forth along
those blue lines into sidings or dead ends, words dreamed up in

that ramshackle grotto, where our father concocted his
alchemical magic. Iodine and magnesium burnt over the sibylline
tripod of the Bunsen burner, its hollow, rasping flame, then
acrid purple smoke that issued forth, as if disclosing prophecy.

A 'cobblers last' served as thunderstone for the finale;
the 'Big Bang'—a scattering of potassium chlorate crystals,
the hammer hit the last—anvil of the elemental gods—
blindingly, the crack and thunder, one incandescent instant,

'the controlled explosion', and behold! a shower of stars;
one galaxy forged in a flash, just as quickly vanished . . .
that blast snapped a snippet of metal off the last's toe;
our father, who played dice with the gods, long before *his* fall.

Beakers, pipettes, rubber hoses, clamps, carboys, stashed
in the bach kitchen cupboard. Here, eldest brother Laurie served
apprenticeship to the Grand Alchemist —cardboard, round
red pill boxes, packed with gunpowder, for Guy Fawkes Day.

All systems of productivity evolve to maximum efficiency.
All systems of productivity evolve, decline, and decay.
If Nothing begat the universe so the universe begat Nothing.
In the beginning, our father, the *Dialectical Materialist*.

Beats the anvil of Lenin: *crime; product of social excess.*
Beats the anvil of Marx: *history repeats; as history then farce.*
Beats the anvil of Trotsky: *revolutions; always verbose.*
Beats the anvil of Engels: *freedom; recognition of necessity.*

'*What the chain?*' The family constantly at war with itself,
'*What the hammer?*' The family acts of aggression unto itself.
'*What the anvil?*' The family psyche imploding upon itself.
Our family, atoms smashing into atoms, '*burning bright*'.

The washhouse stood below the bach. Copper vat set
in a brick kiln (never used) the spring-loaded mangle with vice-
like grip, mounted above the obsolete washing machine,
its toucan beak *click clacking* over two deep, wooden tubs.

Within its high wired, wooden frames, the fowl run held
middle ground. Ancient plum trees gone to wood never fruited.
One old hen for the chopping block. Blunt meat cleaver.
I felt wings stretch for impossible flight under my tenuous

hold, pull taut as sail snapping to wind gust, the headless
thing flopped about the hen house in a bloodied vaudeville act,
and my father quick to scold me for letting go too soon;
pot boiled on the coal range for hours, as tough as old boots.

Those old hens stockpiled eggs in giant mounds anywhere,
under the hen house amidst the piles, that reeked sulphurous if
broken, lumberingly, escaped to roost in the macrocarpa trees
like washing flung loose from the clothesline by the bach.

The ruin of the 'summer house' with green, slatted seating,
slumped forward and never used, slowly collapsing over the years,
under the weight of the passionfruit vine that like the plum or
lemon trees, stalwartly, refused to fruit, antique and talisman.

Mint in a wooden tub to the side of that, behind the lonesome
tap, *drip, dripping*; the one solitary stand of rhubarb, like
some magician's stagey flourish, for the tart dessert I could not
stomach—grew for years on the same spot, shadowy green,

stems flaring dull campfire red; and the lilies that crowded
along the northern boundary, forest thick, created a tunnel to hide
in, or away from an angry pursuer, unseen, scanning corners
by the washhouse and path, to make a calculated run for it.

The long, straight dirt path led *out-the-back* past fowl run
and compost heap (a car packing crate) past the concrete grass
roller (never used) to the ruined, grey sheds riddled with
rat holes, scattered with rusty, useless tools, planked benches.

The bach by the macrocarpa on a winter's night, lisping of
the gas jet heater. Out-the back of our place, one morepork calls
(never seen) from the tallest tree. Pool of yellow lamplight
on my desk. This utter, and abandoned peacefulness, recalled.

Our father *who fell down the porch steps often our father
fell down red concrete steps our father lost his balance liquored
up he was lost his balance and bumped his head our father
did that heaps he did drunken fell and bumped his head now he*

*is dead our father who made our life hell is not in heaven
still maybe falling into the after-nothingness he believed in our
father is still falling for ever and ever our father the bright
young man who matriculated at fourteen star in the ascendant*

*our father the communist our father biochemist and scientist
finally destroyed by the men he trusted our father idealist
Principal of the Pharmacy College Cambridge Terrace Wellington
we watched him sicken and fail and drink himself to death*

*dead at fifty-three he was our father forfeited his life to despair
and the family always flammable blew itself apart like some
laboratory experiment gone horribly wrong in the heart's alembic
none of us escaped strangers at last to each other our father*

*from the King Country the Presbyterian dictum honest day's work
honest day's pay men of the land pragmatic and practical our
father prematurely aged whose father said of his son at his funeral
he should never have left the country our father who art dead.*

GONE: SATIRICAL POEMS: *NEW & SELECTED*

BALLAD OF MISS GOODBAR

Miss Goodbar did bondage to the two-backed beast
with a body decked out like a picnic feast;
turned a few smart tricks every night at least,
    she prayed would last forever.

The neighbours they lamented the noise she made,
and petitioned to get that good lady spayed;
we've all got a particular stock and trade,
    who believe love lasts forever.

They took that petition to the councillor
and rapped loud and long upon his redwood door,
didn't hear him screwing on the parquet floor—
    the world spins on forever.

The weekend rolled on, and the weekend rolled by,
for Janitor Jock had a wandering eye;
slipped on his sneakers and buttoned up his fly,
    whose soul shall burn forever.

Late Sunday night about ten it must have been
not a creature stirred except the streetwise queen—
issued from Miss Goodbar's pad a high pitched scream,
    that echoed on forever.

They called in the coppers with guns on the hips,
they called in the priest with a prayer on his lips;
they dusted down Miss Goodbar for finger-prints—
    and a bed gone cold forever.

Next to her body lay a bunch of brass keys,
not what you'd expect to be the normal fees;
was slit wide open from her neck to her knees—
      the blood flowed on forever.

They took Jock away and they gave him a trial,
then tied him to a chair and fried him awhile—
yet no one could account for that wayward smile,
      frozen on his face forever.

Her first great lover was Christ upon the Cross,
her second-rate lover, an insurance boss—
Miss Goodbar lies tucked in a bed of green moss,
      and there she sleeps forever.

DYLAN THOMAS

A frothy moon and planets wagon deep
as lights slowly lifted on Brown's Hotel
and Dylan leaning there over an ale,
eyes black as coal from an eternal sleep.

'Listen,' he said, 'Some soberly advice,
heavy liquor's for the screaming banshees
avoid the depth charge of double whiskies,
essentially, it's a matter of price.'

The vision faded out to closing time
and the hours peddled a bike down the lane,
the sound of glasses and talk receded.

Awakened now by warblings of a plane
through embankments of cloud into sunshine,
I thought of his tours, how Caitlin pleaded.

BALLADE OF A GLOSSY

In trains by Pymble and Central Station,
in lifts from the first to the second floor,
in brick bungalows throughout the nation,
one can't imagine what they did it for,
in fact, behind every fly screen door,
in cattle pens of the dry Kimberley
women would snicker, sneer, chuckle and roar
and read the *Australian Women's Weekly*.

Our mothers devoured it with a passion
between baking and the latest league score,
what the queen said, who promoted fashion,
did Cary Grant inseminate that whore,
was Grace Kelly upset by a cold sore?
While the winds of change blew but meekly
women pickled and stewed, knuckled and swore
and read the *Australian Women's Weekly*.

To each appetite its daily ration
of sex, beauty, youth and a touch of gore,
the nun, the mutant, the sex slave Martian,
more lies please, it's the truth I abhor.
Whatever the next issue holds in store
it will help to break the monotony
as I scrub and iron and chop and snore
and read the *Australian Women's Weekly*.

Envoy

Now if you contend that life's a bore
pause for a glass of dry, chilled Chianti
to toast Our Lady of Domestic Law,
and read the *Australian Women's Weekly*.

YOU SEE THE ANTHOLOGY MAN

I am you see the anthology man,
very much the fashion, and so today,
I will let you into my little plan.

I adopt a style to seduce the fan;
(one feels *freed* in a familiar way)
I am you see the anthology man.

I shift with fashion, a chameleon,
the man for all seasons, and so today,
I will let you into my little plan.

I am a poseur but of marked *élan*;
(as the ego-gathering tides hold sway)
I am you see the anthology man.

A solipsist does whatever he can,
the devil take the rest, and so today,
I will let you into my little plan.

Any talent challenging me I ban;
(mine is an *exclusive brand* of poesy)
am I you see the anthology man?
I will let you into my little plan.

W.H. AUDEN

Always giving the aerial picture
of the age in which you lived, the odd war
(for this a trip to Iceland served as cure)
your face became the map of metaphor.

Yours pals Spender, MacNeice and Isherwood
agreed that a weed was far too pretty
while the gas tank held the Platonic Good;
beauty you assessed as cause for pity.

Now the Berlin Wall has come tumbling down
and neo-fascist youth is on the rise;
many as gorgeous as the boys you knew.

Narcissus has taken a new disguise
with refugees flooding every town,
that Europe is a mess wouldn't shock you.

LETTER TO JAMES K. BAXTER

An Old Hippie's last trip down the Yellow Brick Road

Man (you're coming across!) I see you
    shamble at a tangent, an ill-dressed shade
heading down to the river, a hairy Esau,
    where Charon is waiting to have you weighed
    to dump your pack, chuck costume aside—
the loosely tied dogma, the pet philosophies
and all the gear made for the mind to tease,

to wrap—made to turn on the status quo.
    Man, across this other side of the border
I throw out my best wishes to the tow
    and for the trip, while time idles, this letter
    to browse as you shift topside for a breather,
knowing the deck hands for a morose mob
without the prospects and without the job.

As distance diminishes Charon's boat
    and the pilot light burns red on the mast,
and the bollard trails on the waters a rope—
    once, twice, the chant for somebody missed:
    heart-dead in Auckland: you answered.
Well, ferrying doesn't turn me on (I fly)
if the Cook Strait is anything to go by.

Rain overhead, and that reminds me—
    an acre of roof to tar, brush and paint
in the few week days left that are sunny.
    Far out, I'll trust to luck my patron saint
    till the weather shows some sign of restraint;
the hour moves on, I've a busy schedule,
I scratch on my sleeve: LOVE IS PRACTICAL.

A jaunt by boat that isn't headed far,
    two or three hours at most—and a sunset.
Likewise, five minutes on a cable car
    is about as much as I'm prepared to take.
    And walking (the risk of arriving late)
is, above all, the way I take my travel;
or that's how I grooved when I was single.

Married now, I'm given over to the itch
    for travel, for the foreign scenery,
tossing for a change we bought two tickets
    left the *Black Swans of Pāuatahanui*
    (we rented a shack there) chose the red clay,
the chillier climate, we moved south:
marriage as a gamble sometimes pays off.

2.

Hell is forever the season of Fall:
    each instant, a million souls burst aflame
as *The Omnipotent* deems them combustible,
    least, so that heavy, the firebrand Calvin
    drummed in (the vibrations reached Dunedin),
hard to buy that those salamanders
burn, screech and sizzle like Lowell's spiders.

Hell is a tourist kick, a flag on the map
    set up by Christian control (not the AA).
The transport is hip, the climate is hot,
    enticements abound for the *émigré*
    as added incentive to the journey;
spectacular billboards boast the Good Life
that means no hardship, man, no nagging wife.

Hell is slick as any big business:
   marketing is sound, the budget's not mean
thanks to a well-briefed board of directors
   the company clubs and the research team,
   and, sure, the superannuation scheme.
Clients are taught (they pay a rip-off fee)
not all fishes come from the Holy See.

A bout of dirty weather up ahead—
   I'm pretty sure I heard a howling dog
the wind coming strong (he'll wake the dead)
   just where is it all at—and this fog!
   The boat, river, crew (and dog) obscured:
and that mist, thick as hallucination.
Maybe, man, hell is your destination?

3.

We pay our dues to the product well made:
   I observe your face scrawled on the mist-air
you're big business, your image has paid.
   Passing by a shop front window I saw—
   and this vision put me on a downer,
your face, impressed (bloodless) on a towel;
a trendy / cotton / quasi / vernicle.

But don't get off on this rave of mine
   if I show how they're stealing your thunder.
You're a commodity, you're big time,
   you've made it, you're a commercial number;
   yeah, I bet it grabs your sense of humour.
Though popular, I better let you know
you never sold fast as the Rev. Bob Lowe.

You (we know) made it with the apathetic,
    the druggie, the dropout, the hippie
the lesbian, and, the alcoholic,
    the queer and the (could I call you Hemi?)
    You had an ear for everyman's story.
Too bad you didn't get time to hear mine.
I'll add that to the letter in a later rhyme.

You're added like a fact to our nation
    by which I mean the corporate image,
so you get, man, a standing ovation
    giving rise to the thing: CONSCIOUSNESS.
    By a cool twist of metamorphosis
you became the body and blood of a metaphor—
we don't knock it, it was you held the floor.

A people—we just haven't the stability
    that flows by the banks of time and custom;
the hourly news teaches us our history.
    What's not practical equals a big yawn;
    DIY pretty much is rule of thumb.
We don't own a national saint—but cheer
that oddball: the *Sportsman of the Year*.

Wasn't it Glover said at your wake—
    it wouldn't be long before they gave you
the rank that will set you up as a saint?
    No King George Medal, no Olive Laurel,
    just beatitudes and a plastic halo:
Campbell didn't trust you with his women
till you creek-jumped to Catholicism.

Yet I don't want to blow your trip,
   certainly don't want to be, *ah*, pharisaical;
even as your corporeal light (dig it)
   dims to dust and I warm to a parable
   we hear the priest grooving on a moral.
Meantime, the apologists are freaked for fun:
God / Man / Poet? Maybe all three in one?

The *Big Stone of Respectability*
   blocks us in, it's a mountain to be moved.
Some few have the strength and agility,
   fewer still know where to find a handhold.
   You shoved it free and tightened the blindfold,
put on a sheepskin (maybe gabardine?)
You walked that plank across the lion's den.

And, *so what!* if you were messianic:
   but never extreme, man, never militant,
though if it rose on the mind graph: panic:
   you flogged it back with a buckle belt
   the stinging reminder given with each welt,
you weren't Christ. Who was that Irishman
wrapped himself in chains to do the same?

4.

Now it's autumn. Under the shadow
   the garden craps out (no hope for the corn),
I study the hedge and watch the holes grow;
   my son drags his wooden bee on the lawn.
   Yeah man, remember that ancient scene
when I showed you my first funky sonnets:
ornate as old dames in flowery bonnets.

Enclosed is a pic. of where we're living;
    hope it isn't crumpled in the mail,
in the foreground grows the *hedge-in-a-ring*.
    Uterine: but on a much larger scale;
    get the focus, it's not too bad at all!
To the left out of view stands the tannery;
owning your own shack—that means money.

Let me take a trip back to childhood:
    to slow up the frames, point out the scene
on how I inched up (don't mean babyhood)
    the infant in his exultant Eden—
    too much footage for this introduction;
I'll skip the scene of the catapult club
or how I plumbed manhood inside a pub.

Example: two quick flashes come to light
    grandpa Lou's *artificial foot* in a cupboard,
when he died, mother kept it by right—
    the family held things, they used to hoard.
    Instance: biscuits decayed in tins long stored.
I remember, too, when someone's mongrel
broached the hencoop, shredded every fowl.

I soon clicked 'Life' ran to a new rule—
    something shifted, freed long frozen locks,
I began to turn on, to use my cool;
    pre-puberty pink and lime green socks!
    The mid-fifties had me by the bollocks.
Coolly slipping between the parent and state,
pop culture became my new playmate.

I came on the tail end of Haley's Comets,
   Rock 'n' Roll (tree fort days and a rope swing!)
Can't have been much more than five or six.
   Not long after, came beatniks and brylcreem,
   after the craze died on Johnny Devlin.
Between times I read a heap of Zane Grey;
I dream the purple sage to this very day.

With slick kiss-curl my eldest brother
   kept right up on the hottest of the rock,
the radio with built-in record player
   spun the plastic platters of the *top pop:*
   Buddy Holly, Fabian (but he was a flop).
Then came that dynamo of pelvic energy,
the Great King of Rock 'n' Roll: Elvis Presley.

Didn't have any quiet upbringing—
   four brothers and a sister made competition
one hell-of-a-lot more bitching than singing,
   so I took up with the music revolution
   to find an emotional Plimsoll line ...
learning to daydream in an electronic noise,
that became one of my favourite ploys.

5.

Yo! Interactive communication:
   a world hard-wired to the DJ patter,
the satellite, the transmitter station—
   (way before the world of email chatter)
   succinct as any play by Pinter;
our condition—I don't mean to be heavy,
remains that of a scrambled sensibility.

Don't get the idea I'm out of my head
   sending up this game, the age we live in,
(*stuff it!* where we lie we make our bed)
   can't get off on the Great Illumination—
   like tuning in to the days of Marsden,
can't charter discoveries like one poet;
exhilaration won't fire from my musket!

Illumination? The poet's got to act:
   so he decides to give identity,
to our small history, spiritual fact.
   He sets caulking a poem on discovery
   to build an ark for New Zealand Poetry.
One temptation we should deny ourselves
is to reach for bickie tins on high shelves.

Before I get onto art and all that,
   I'll move on to sketch the community
of youth, and about where my story's at,
   (on my list this gets top priority)
   in the section marked: Autobiography.
I must have stopped growing some years ago,
I'm still about 5'6" from head-to-toe.

O to escape the great urban sprawl—
   away from the paranoia of conurbation;
I still remember as a kid at school
   walking hills now boxed in sub-division—
   who can ramble a quarter acre section?
Within a month you'd see a new smoke stack
turn the sky dirty as a shook coal sack.

Wellington: 'city of the soulless'
   or so you reckoned, too bad, I think of
buildings high as wheat on those husky hills
   as a stamping ground, as my home city;
   a scene you knocked about as a postie.
I packed up my books and pots, greased the car
and one bleak hour split on the *Aramoana*.

6.

The '60s announced open house:
   in city and suburb the word then spreading
to the lost and fallen and unloved youth.
   Dribs to droves meant columns migrating—
   this was the start, the age of communing;
press and parent couldn't bring back children
who flocked to your call: *Jerusalem!*

Then the pseudo spiritualism hit:
   all things eastern: Krishna, Buddha and Zen,
Jesus freaks mobilised aboard a truck;
   home spun neo-existentialism—
   how to exorcise that incubus, Time.
Sure enough, the emotion went out of it;
from those ashes cheers the New Socialite.

Anyway, I escaped it. You could say
   I didn't turn myself onto that game—
socially. I was uncool, I was shy;
   sternly taught to greet folk by surname,
   note my style yet retains a formal stain.
Right on! it didn't take long for novelty
to roll the joint of respectability.

What did it man? The sun taper thin
    calling you from autumn Dunedin, or
leaves thick as manuscripts in the Octagon.
    Maybe some hassle, some domestic law—
    promptings that pushed you out the door?
Groovy—how I'd dig to do that, a gas
to leave behind me my *bourgeois* shit house.

PS:

I spun out. The house? that's behind me,
    garden, wife, the kid, and all the rest.
I headed North again to hit the home city
    with a bumper load of books (only the best).
    How many Steads can fit in a tea chest?
That's how it went man, I left real quick. *Yeah!*
with HARDY, CHAUCER, THE BIBLE, SHAKESPEARE.

THE LOVER

A touch of charm and total attention
was one device which assured his success
with women though he tended to excess;
those over forty don't rate a mention.

Although he considered the kiss a bore
the flash cars and *Glenfiddich* did the trick;
generous to a fault, tacky and slick,
he sought in each the virgin and the whore.

His love was as abstract as fantasy:
the preceding lovers and how they screwed,
we assume he dredged the female psyche.

Yet all of them outgrew him by a feud;
after the parties and pornography
they found him sad and obvious—not lewd.

DOCTOR ROCK

Sounding a sonnet for B.J. & Associates

He accumulated fans each new shift:
punk, reggae, indie, maybe some swamp rock,
pumped hip-hop and Motown and techno rift;
he timed the hits to the top of the clock—

while every other night of the week
sorted the hot-spots and the top-shelf tart:
and though he figured as the total freak
could work the women with a salesman's art.

Sexual conquests confirmed the cliché,
the white convertible, black top, the blonde
caught the marble eyed gaze of the DJ;
without a doubt he felt that he belonged.

The cowboy: *Drifter on the fm Band?*
give him his due, the drugs and one night stand.

MISS LILY

for Matt Ottley

Let me tell an odd tale
    about Miss Eliza Lily,
she came from the western suburbs
    of a harbourside city.

Miss Lily, *Dear Lady*—
    and Wacky, the cockatoo!
shared a drab, rickety mansion,
    (walled garden and outdoor loo).

By most considered short
    at fifteen hands from head to floor,
she measured in the order of—
    let's say about five-foot-four.

One thing deserves mention
    like the ancient *Irish Elk* long dead
earned Miss Lily notoriety—
    a pair of hands grew on her head.

A dab hand on the harpsichord
    she played the Bandicoot Serenade,
Wacky on the breadboard beat time
    and danced the harlequinade.

She'd pose as the shaggy moose
    that ambled round mountain lakes,
she hid out back in Huon pine
    by the garden shed and rakes.

Her fame grew increasingly,
    you might say by public pranks—
she'd take off to the oddest spots
    via bus stops and taxi ranks.

In the Hilton Hotel foyer
    she'd often pose as a hatstand
freaking out the *maître d'hôtel,*
    next to the baby white grand.

She'd hike to the domain
    if the sky whipped up a storm,
she'd catch lightning bolts in her hand
    and hurl them about the lawn.

On Sundays she liked best
    to play ball on the Oval Green—
she used those hands to good effect
    as backstop to a baseball team.

The bus to Maggie's Market
    ran to time but the time ran slow;
Miss Lily counted red brick villas
    by liver brick row upon row.

Melons and muffins she picked
    enough to fill a wicker basket,
Wacky meanwhile hissed and spat
    on cats at Maggie's Market.

Late at night she loved to jump
    and flap her hands as birds in flight,
under the lilac moon would sing
    delirious with delight.

Alert as a satellite dish
    the hands sprouting on her head;
the dolphin and the dugong sang
    lullabies to her in bed.

O Miss Lily's golden hair
    glowed fiery in the setting sun,
she shared the secrets of the forests
    with boys and girls just for fun.

She told them of medicines
    in rainforests under a curse,
she told them of bark and berries
    that cured Asian flu or worse.

She told them of rivers
    that flowed to a silver lagoon,
she told them of the far away seas
    that rolled to the lilac moon.

One night the sky grew dark
    then black and even blacker still,
Miss Lily sent the children home
    as the wind blew loud and shrill.

It howled on into the night
    and the steeple bells rang madly,
it knocked chimney pots into streets
    and behaved very badly.

High up on Mount Wellington
    pylon cables came crashing down;
the one sole source of energy
    in that storm-tossed harbour town.

They called out civil defence
    who considered themselves the best,
they even called out the bowling club
    who woefully proved a pest.

The town mayor threw a fit
    and the councillors heaved a sob,
the townsfolk had enough and cried:
    PUT MISS LILY ON THE JOB!

She took the broken cables—
    clenched them in both her hands,
she fused the cable ends together
    where the lonely pylon stands.

She lit up like some beacon
    much brighter than a movie star,
household lights came streaming on
    and the mayor shouted the bar.

So by public vote all agreed:
    ERECT A STATUE OF MISS LILY.
If she considered this *déclassé*
    Wacky didn't think it silly.

In the gallery she now stands,
    a sandstone slab in the Great Hall:
her hands clasped above her head
    next to the wombat Big as a Bull.

Billy and his babe, armed, up on the roof,
appears at this distance, well—quite aloof;
one bullet drills headmaster through the eye,
his gown flutters, he flops like a magpie.
She cocks one leg like a stork and giggles,
puts a hand on her hip, pouts and wiggles;
'*Oh, neat one Billy! Another dead bod,*
I say, there's quite a pile down in the quad.'
Matron by the oak, dashes for the door,
too late!—her tartan skirt splattered in gore.
That fat kid, bailed up, holding in his tum,
is gutshot, why he's screaming for his mum.
The chaplain holds up his crucifix, begs
them to stop, but cops one between the legs.
Billy dreams he's in a computer game
against his will and every day's the same;
enough! enough! enough! enough! enough!
He has no future, couldn't give a stuff—
gets a head in his sights, sees it explode;
takes the girl from behind and blows his load.
This is the world then, what it has become;
therefore, let us rejoice—evil's great fun!

BALLAD OF THE TAJ MAHAL

A restaurant with fountain and water clock
comprised one plan for a shut down toilet block—
domed like a mosque, chained, under padlock;
       enshrined as the Taj Mahal.

Years long and rusty this privy stood disused,
many a gland, they say, was here defused;
such gentlemen taken short were not amused—
       preyed on at the Taj Mahal.

Came here the councillors plans to invent,
they prayed that success would be heaven sent;
but know their bowels were as thrifty as Lent,
       squatting in the Taj Mahal.

The saturated walls soon gave short shrift
to new laid plans when the precincts were sniffed—
many shed a tear over schemes gone adrift,
       to jazz up the Taj Mahal.

A smart Greek suggested a drive-in car wash,
so why go down-market when you can go posh?
It's all one to derros—they don't give a toss,
       pissing on the Taj Mahal.

Oh, the writing, it's certain, was on the wall,
though not all such sentiments were shared by all—
still, drains will gurgle after heavy rainfall,
       in troughs by the Taj Mahal.

If the walls of Jericho fell to the trumpet;
know that these will stand or fall on their merit,
no matter what gay boy sets out to mourn it—
         lost days at the Taj Mahal.

Some dream of precious stones from far away,
some of amethyst, or onyx with pearl inlay,
some of greenstone from down Hokitika way;
         to brighten the Taj Mahal.

If fire engines scream, and the traffic roars by,
and walls have ears, though you cannot guess why—
take a glass of Chablis beneath a domed sky,
         to salute the Taj Mahal.

'Taj Mahal' Public Toilets (Former)
Cambridge Terrace and Kent Terrace, WELLINGTON

BALLADE OF THE POSTER

Whatever event you wish to display,
on walls or billboards, any space at all,
posters to promote a movie or play,
some carnival, band, parade, or football;
on telegraph poles, bus stops, city mall,
posters on Main Street, in every café,
not forgetting the Community Hall,
and I think I'll go postering today!

Poster art arose under Jules Chéret,
in the Belle Époque, when as I recall,
Toulouse-Lautrec enjoyed *femme déclassée*,
a funny little man but no one's fool,
for his poster art was the best of all;
rain threatens, I'm ready for my foray
(I left my staple gun on a bar stool),
and I think I'll go postering today!

I've pasted all the way to San Jose,
I've pasted boulevards and City Hall,
I've pasted down by the Dock of the Bay,
I've pasted prairies and heard the call,
poster flora for the concrete jungle;
I was wild with a paste broom in my day,
still I abide by that one simple rule,
and I think I'll go postering today!

Envoy

Feel the bustle & hum the city pull,
the weather might turn so I won't delay,
I love the outdoors yet I hated school,
and I think I'll go postering today!

BALLAD OF A YOBBO

Barry, dead keen on feral boar,
hunted that beast, then he killed it.
His .44 Magnum made the hit:
semi-auto action with a big bore.

He worked the circuit as stockman
up North, way back in his youth,
'what a great life that was—streuth!'
A good pair of boots and a fry pan.

Friday night's soak in the tub:
hair slicked back with old pig fat—
Barry donned a broad-brim hat,
and off he went to trash some pub.

On women he had a basic view
shared with mates by the stock pen:
'can't fuck 'em, chuck rocks at 'em'
he bluntly stated, stirring the stew.

Something spooked Barry lately,
was it the tucker or lumpy bed?
Something weird got into his head,
nightmares troubled him greatly.

First he blamed it on bad plonk,
he sank a few before hitting the sack
(a bottle of bourbon in his pack);
maybe he fancied a drunken bonk?

Demons had him by the balls—
it appeared he slowly decomposed;
this'll end badly, he supposed,
demons don't play Aussie rules.

Barry turned *Australopithecus:*
one cranky bloke on a short fuse,
years spent sculling the booze
sealed his fate with a deadly kiss.

His mates said it'd gone too far—
Barry collapsed in a bloody heap
as if hit by a road train in his sleep;
they sold him off to an abattoir.

Nightly, those gruesome dreams,
morphing into a pile of pig gut.
Shovelled into buckets onto a truck,
branded dog food on TV screens.

'Yobbomeat' stamped on the can,
'Tasty Tucker A Dog Loves To Eat'.
The Ads aired on Sesame Street,
a dog's best friend—Barry the man!

GONE

Uncle Barny lived with us at our place.
For him the war was a bloody good show.
Yet though it all ended some time ago,
as the spitfire ace he made the skies safe.

Kettles shriek in every suburban house.
Someone plays an oboe in some back room
a half-forgotten, half remembered tune;
I hate my job, it croons, I hate my spouse.

The sun rolls westward on its rusty rim.
Dusk dulls into pewter. Streetlights come on.
From the radio drifts a winsome song—
the evening primrose, the lawns cut trim.

Next to the brickyard and misty canal
a school teacher peddles by lost in thought.
Carpet slippers, a pipe, one glass of port,
but a factory whistle breaks the spell.

Lanes fade off into countryside unseen.
Beyond city limits chugs one freight train.
At the last terrace and storm water drain
trucks crawl behind a hay baling machine.

It's better not to know what lies ahead.
We used to believe that the world was flat,
now belief in God seems pretty old hat.
Live for the moment is what Horace said.

Public Libraries everywhere shut down,
from Newcastle, Grimsby, to Kensal Rise.
What with electronics, no big surprise—
it spreads like a virus from town to town.

Time accumulates like dust on a mat—
old gasworks by the tavern block the view,
a popular spot for the post pub screw;
but in the end we grew quite sick of that.

NO ONE KNOWS

No one knows what goes on inside my head,
one thought chases another one away;
least, that is what I think the Master said.

Some days I prefer to stay tucked in bed,
mood swings often as not take me that way:
no one knows what goes on inside my head.

Fear that erupts like gamma rays I dread;
such are those demons that lead one astray,
least, that is what I think the Master said.

One must work hard to keep the ego fed,
would that we were gods at the close of day:
no one knows what goes on inside my head.

That heavy footfall is the devil's tread,
quit the premises now—do not delay;
least, that is what I think the Master said.

You did not notice the neighbours had fled
who disappeared before the break of day.
No one knows what goes on inside my head,
least, that is what I think the Master said.

POETRY DAY BLUES

So; let's wheel out the laureates
with ornately carved walking sticks,
Huey, Dewey, Dopey. Grumpy.
Yay! it's National Poetry Day.
Awards for faction and fiction,
for fancy postmodern diction;
books on pies, and poems and puns.
Books on boats, bivouacs, and buns,
books about hubcaps, hiccups, bumps,
books on measles (the odd lumps).
There's the *Knife-In-The-Back Award*,
(I'm sure that's one I can't afford).
The senses spin, but what to choose?
That good ol' poetry lovin' blues.
Don't give up yet, oh, don't despair,
help is at hand for help is near.
Go ask *Snow White*—that babe knows
just which way the cool wind blows;
judge exemplar, queen of chick lit,
the rule-of-thumb *apparatchik*.
Poems about bagels, ladders, bikes,
poems praising porn, and diesel dykes.
Poems on pavements, poems on walls,
poems at bus stops, poems in halls.
The true (a few) the old, the fake,
a posse of poets—make or break.

NIGHT

Opposite me two poets snore and fart,
   hurtling down the highway, pedal to floor.
A sordid night's jaunt in the name of art;
   one poet's a ponce, the other's a bore.
Against the graffiti wall leans a tart,
   the meter clicks over, keeping the score.
Our driver silent, still, playing his part.
   Opposite me two poets fart and snore. . . .

One violently retches, soon settles down.
   Night coagulates, behind us the town
in the rear vision mirror, postcard size;
   harbour lights throw up another high rise.
Neon bluely fizzes, the night is raw. . . .
   Opposite me two poets fart and snore.

A satire addressing the Rupert Brooke
sonnet 'Dawn' written in the early 1900s

LUXEMBOURG

THE MAP

Atrocious snow blanketed the village.
Only the rounded portals of yellow
light indicated where windows had been.
One skeletal church spire rose above
the laden rooftops. Alpine valleys blurred
under plush darkness, the fossilized,
soft contours of this night bound place.
In the market square, the *clerici vagantes*
declared that ego had collapsed under
its own weight, subsided into the sinkhole
of self-adulation; poets were complicit,
they said, the mind finally turned wolf
and consumed its young, language bowed
before an absurdist code of linguistics.

Twilight of the Anthropocene Age:
we soon deluded ourselves in the belief
that panic did not exist by pursuing
rational exegesis, systematic amassing of
information superseded the biomass.
A false sense of security prevailed
in cities that promised little beyond what
was known, the tuneless instruments
of lyricists now cast aside, administration
blocks amplified the hollow breath
of air conditioning—clack of keyboards.
Barbarism grew rank in desert regions,
mountain fastnesses, across borderlands;
raw recruits convened as death cults.
Terror and tribalism, enmeshed in mortal
combat, waged war against pluralism
and the present for a mediaeval caliphate

that never existed, as if time played
itself back somehow, and paradise shone
retrospectively.

                    Time stretched
like tendons of an overworked athlete.
'Was memory a dangerous place?'
He marked it out on the map, got as far
as the snow line, and there he rested,
cigarette aglow, staring into the distance.
Cold played upon him, in the way that
a harmonica recalls pond stillness.
He died where he squatted, eyes held the
same fixed stare that he had in life;
pupils dilated as the sun contracted west,
his face, momentarily, a golden mask.

They wore thick leather jerkins. I can't recall the colour, oak brown, or maybe black. The men lumbered like some slow choreographed minstrel show (or mediaeval procession), with giant sacks slung over their backs (bent) round the back of our place to dump the broken load in the cut down packing case that served to house the heaped up coal. The coal man, sometimes two in single file, stooped, heavy stepped, in foul weather or fine, past our kitchen window. Year in year out they filed by, to feed the wetback coal range, which like some leviathan at home in its bay, occasionally breached, sending a spume of steam hissing and bubbling angrily from the roof overflow pipe, only to subside and exhale with a repeated, regurgitant, gasping. Taciturn, stolid men. I dared not speak to them, but only saw their hunched forms on a migratory track they could not seemingly be deflected from. The Anthropolite Man who lived amongst the seams in a world of gleaming, oily shale, tattooed maybe with fronds and ferns from extinct tropical forests, in spirals that could no longer be deciphered.

UNDERCOVER

The moon was half. As though the act
of clearing a space in the partially clouded
sky had worn itself away. In the ceiling,
at the eastern corner, above the bathroom,
there under the broken eave, a starling
has made her nest—scraping and pecking
well into the night. I would have preferred a
thrush, well-bred and shy, though they
have their quarters happily and secretly
secured in a place I do not know of.
And, ubiquitously, the 'timid temerity' of
the sparrow riotous in a thickly leafed
camellia bush, up against the neighbour's
house, by the dozen, a noisy senate,
the day's activities under discussion, by the
last of the deflected heat off that brick wall.
An Ongarue truck and trailer from the
quarry grinds down the hill past my thickening
barricade of bush and shrub—I get a glimpse,
in part, as it passes along the gaps between.

A Fonterra milk truck and trailer, elongated
and oval, flashes its chrome silver bright,
(white gold flooding the nation's coffers)
and grinds up the hill past my place.
Absent twenty years, I left a country of sheep,
returned to a country of cattle; rivers
wheeze through an iridescent landscape,
gorged on nutrient-rich run off. This is *lower
socio-economic* territory round here in the
North King Country; run-down rentals
and mouldering hatreds, hobbled by small
town boredoms. It's pretty, looking out
over the valley at dusk, to the hills, seeing

all the lights of the town laid out brilliant
as LA. But this isn't LA. This is rural New
Zealand, where every woman over forty
looks like Janet Frame in a parallel universe,
of the underprivileged. This is a scene
set for the opening of a Western; the danger,
and the standoff; and that is as far as
it gets. As though the locals had lost the script,
or the plot, not sure what move to make
next—if indeed there is ever a next.
The entire rehearsal eddies to nothingness.
But, *what happens* next (and folk will admit to
this), is nothing more nor less than weather.

GREEN ASTERISK

It is the way out of town, north, over the railway
lines polished by a hundred tyres every hour year upon year,
by rolling stock for longer still, chugging the decades,
clanging the crossings of every small town on the
                    Main Trunk Line

where the light runs quicksilver, this way and that,
along the rails. Is this your destination then—why north?
A bigger city warmed by money and all the lust that
want brings, no longer holds the same attractions,
as if it ever did. Necessity has replaced hunger.
One always returns not because it is home, for there is
no other place to go.

            They rise to view, Pirongia Mountain,
Maungatautari, as I pass between them, heading north.
A brand new yellow 4 Square Store lights up main street,
short and wide.

            Bungalows set back amongst
elegant gardens and rough-hewn, stylish stone walls, suggest
that these districts might well be called counties; Waipa,
Waikato, Franklin whose dairy farmers sing the praises of
curds and whey all the way to the bank.

            The wives lack a
city, money gives them privilege, protection, which clears
a space round them, empty ownership of air. A cabbage tree
pins its green asterisk to the ridgeline.

An hour on this back road loops back,
the pull of State Highway 1, heading north at Ngāruawāhia.
The Waikato river running dead silent alongside; road,
rail, and the river seemingly abandoned, its surface
a pummelled pewter.

Behind you the copper tinged, cattle-bowed paddocks.
Blockish silhouettes. Cubist installations propped there under
a question mark of trees.

To the city as particle accelerator.
                    You draw to that magnet under a
passing squall, and those ink blotches across the windscreen
are tree crowns seen through rain.

To that coastal city flat on its circular rim at the end
of this battering ram highway, embossed as a warrior's shield,
or bright and young as a rubbish tin lid.

THE DEPARTED GUEST

His skull is an abandoned amphitheatre,
empty of echoes, the green tinge to the inner
cavity his last twilight dream of ancient forests.

And here, follow the traces of the two weathers
that afflicted his dreams: *hope*: that always
meant the future, and: *fear*: the drone of a past
that could never be undone.

                    Over time,
the parietal plates of his skull drifted apart,
the Pangaea of his centre, constructs of his thought,
set out in a system of the rationale, all fell softly
aside, without so much as a whisper.

Decomposition began from the inside out,
unhurriedly, merciless and unstoppable as rumour.
That other, the one within him,
                              departed the bastion
of his being, silently, and without his knowledge.

ROAD NOTES

'The traveller is the aggregate of the road.'
          —Antonio Machado

III
Flat bottom clouds. Paperweights.
Slide above the horizon on wires and pulleys
realistic as false scenery.

V
One sooty white horse standing alone in
a paddock, still as a plaster cast.

VI
One lone container dumped beyond the farm
gate, under the copse, squat as a bandit's bungalow.

VIII
A convocation of cabbage butterflies
dance out of focus, whitely, across State Highway I.
Over the Bombay Hills.

XIV
Velvet sheen is maize stubble, combed back
in lit rows, as I head north, buzz cut back from sunrise
to sunset. Paddocks either side. Autumn litter.

XV
A portion of this paddock slopes to a pine grove.
Memory has pulled tent pegs and moved on.
A sadness of light all that remains, the mould broken.

XVIII

Between the mile-high voices of adults to
unruly mood states I had never known—
that road sculpted by the confines of the day.

XXII

High beam hauls in the white line;
the Milky Way, its skid mark slung across the sky,
runs out of steam.

XXIII

The Huntly Power Station under drizzle.
Overlord of the river. A mediaeval shadow block.
Dilapidated cottages thrown about its base.

XXVI

Mid-summer. High green staves of poplars,
even when stilled, look wind washed. The *en plein air*
artist who painted them has just left.

XXX

Green glow of paddocks
iridescent as a Petri dish. Mezzanine floor of mist
over autumn valleys, roadside.

THIS WAY OUT

In the fossil record is found no remnant
of the body's soft tissues, these things melt
away, substances by which we sense
ourselves; petrified bone and the catacombs
that riddle bone remain. The rest melted
away. What we were awaits to be uplifted
by some mountain range yet to be born.
Pressed as if some marker between sheets of
schist we become geology. Our home a
mountain axis. Prevailing winds the gathered
breath of ourselves and all our dead.
Such thoughts are composed of solitudes.
Startled, we drop back through the trapdoor
of dream in endless S-curves chasing the
far distant notes of Orpheus as he plays
so high and sweet on his moon bone flute.

Goshawk lands upon the glove with the shock of recognition. We have supplanted the God with ego. After that, it's downhill all the way into invention, great works of art, the ghost of immortality. Sanguine and blinkered attempts to reach past illusion, stave off oblivion. Does anything possess value if we do not bestow value upon it?

O taxonomy of desperation, catalogue of doubt. The imperative that we must not know in order to discover. Humankind's belief system at work. Love, too? The greatest deception of all. The naked self, teetering on the brink of the precipice. Vulnerability meets impending loss.

One man falling off a cliff will clutch at any inaccessible flower in an attempt to stop his fall. That's love for you—grasping at the impossible, hope without foundation. Regret means floating, not falling. Lament also the dismantling of language, lexicon of the poet who falters and fails into obscurantism. That construct wherein ego reigns supreme, declamatory testament to Narcissus, deflected off the burnished shield. Post-structuralists hectoring from Babel's tower drowned in binary codes. In the eye-blink of hawk time accelerates to a still point at the moment of impact.

HOUSE OF OCCLUSION

after reading Tatiana Shcherbina

Left open long enough spiders will weave these
windows shut, then my world would become a web,
as though I were peering back through old age
as if through gauze, not knowing if that glimmer lies
behind or ahead of me. So I consider my imagined
blindness from plan view. Is focus an inward,
or outward speculation on this house of occlusion?
Spider spells it out in web letters, by a lexicon of
intersections, through hollow-eyed caves of the dead.
'Buried in our lives we are governed by ghosts.'
My windowsills remain a battleground, bits thrown
about, shattered insignia of the housefly abound.
Yellow and crimson grains of sunset make an altar,
as the oblatory spider pays fully the lares et penates.

The white moon, a wild mare, driven into the canyon, clouds churned beneath its hooves; toadstools in pine plantations accumulate, some grubby little act performed late at night; green and crinkled, the sheep-terraced hills, white and pink, the purple magnolia bloom.

One singular, brick chimney stack rigid as any branding iron, silent as an exclamation mark. The orbiting, ghost of a house. Beneath and through a copse of native bush, the stream tumbled out of sight, descending into a narrow gorge under the limestone bluff. Looking down from a backcountry road, the whole seen in miniature, suggestive of some pastoral scene not unlike this one. Overall, the sense not of loss but absence.

Once upon a time—but what of it? Nothing happened, no beginnings, endings fizzled out after a few false starts. No discernible joy and even less despair. Nothing happened of any consequence. No fairies at the bottom of the garden, no goblins in the glade.

No agape amongst the livestock; birth and death notices ascended in dizzying columns and as quickly dispersed, like chimney smoke, into nothingness. Dark matter into oblivion. The stream that echoed through the narrow gorge increased and diminished in volume, much as expected, and according to the seasons.

THE WAITING

After rain, a still evening, the gathering dark,
cloud cover a grey-blue. Quietness. Starter engine
of the morepork. A test run. Soon, the full-
throated, measured call from high up on the hill,
behind this house, itself an engine room of
sorts, gently reshuffling in its frame, the air cools,
floorboards creak with the footpads of ghosts,
the fridge digestibly, chirrups, and exhales.
The low hum of a car, unseen, passes on through
the night, lengthening along the valley road.
Darkness thickens. The waiting. Deeper quiet.
And still the morepork has not sounded its first,
questioning call at this hour. One dog barks
at some backyard swing standing still as a gibbet.

Every distraction arrives complete, absorbs
our adoration. This is it. Till again, boundaries
blur distances, shuffle like ash. Another ego
burn off. The orchards of the soul might have
illuminated a monk's dream, his cell sweetened
by the honey of his God. The desert air blown
so dry it crackles, like wind at the entrance to a
cave; open-mouthed, and silent as any cry of
faith. His palms brush one against the other for
loss and for love. He knows that in the dark,
the stars will rage with light, that the margins of
the Psalms will once again be transformed
into marble columns set aglow by his thought.

An old story. Our hero wakes up disoriented in a strange and unfamiliar land. Rock strewn, treeless. He is amnesiac; expulsion from Eden is false memory. The Ruskinesque, quartz blaze of a fallen rock. Into his field of vision float half erased memories. The plank hulled ship stretched upon the leek green sea, for instance. Though how did he get here? Balloon cheeked clouds puff powdery gusts from every quarter. The ship tilts toward its destiny, sails pot-belled and proud. An empire in red shading and black lines spell out emptiness. A clutch of minuscule palm trees lean toward the coast. A few towns and oases marked out phonetically in copperplate promise little. Inland remains largely terra incognita, a persistent rumour. He observes a lizard, frozen beneath his shadow, its back patterned with yellow chevrons. This reminds him of ship's anchors. The map fades off, borderless, into obscurity. The horizon swings on its boom in one slow arc either side of the perpendicular. The emissary has not yet returned with news from the ant-headed people. At best, trade routes remain speculative. Twilight is the texture of wickerwork all around him. Soon the stars.

STILL LIFE WITH BOULDERS

Oparure Road, Waitomo

Not quite stubble, more the plucked flesh of fowl,
after the maize harvest, cut to the grain, close cropped
paddocks. An April sun draws shadows across the land,

velvety black, thick as sump oil, the air glass bright,
though filtered as if the light voltage had dimmed, but
nothing as definite as that, except for the sliding

partitions that are invisible, so that the plucked flesh
has become crew cut paddock, and barely a minute gone.
The scene slipping by seemingly so ancient every second

caught up in an eternity of stillness, and the light that
lacquers the surface of everything, shiny as an iridescent
backed beetle on line-after-line of maize stubble,

in the slow, wondrous tilt of the earth, barely audible
yet felt—each valley holds its own set of mediaeval ruins,
as if one fortified town had fallen one after the other,

reduced to foundations of stacked limestone, half buried,
boulders strewn over hillsides, loosed from some
trebuchet; violence long since returned to the underworld.

THE WORLD'S BASEMENT

The secret lies in memory forgotten; to look
forward is to view perception within the mirror,
staring back, shock of journeys taken, buried.
Everything forgotten is what you know,

has been done, continuously, stumbling back
through the mirror, broken, bleeding light.
Night appalls with its slow, dragging weight,
Lethe-wards slide into sleep; crocodile hours.

Once, within a wadi in the Sinai desert, I heard
the echo in the rock—startling against silence,
as if Orpheus played upon his harp soundlessly,
his touch so exquisite you sensed the sound

all around; that he had never ceased singing his
music, filling the world's basement to overflowing.

The hydrologists were unanimous—not all rivers flowed to the sea. Many had stalled. River mouths and estuaries silted. The mightiest of them grown sluggard (the river in a coffin) inched in eddies, trending sou'west, opened its palm arthritically to the sea. Transmontane systems yet made a show of it, garbled through gravel, under bridges, pushed coastward. There were no 'rivers great and fine / of oil, milk, honey and wine' as heralded by the wandering scholars who laughed loudly at the afterlife.

The unveiling of The Temple of the Sacred Cow, a cacophony of pump and filter, rose twenty storeys chrome bright, overlooked vast river plains to the north, garlands of pennyroyal heaped at its base. Along the horizon, high risers (fallen angels) glowed incandescent into the night as if they had stolen fire from the heavens. What of those river gods and creatures celebrated in bestiaries? Scouting parties of laboratory technicians took samples from tributary and anabranch; found no indicators for marine life, only ample evidence of emptiness.

WORRY BEADS

If there were no God I would pray for the things
I have ceased to believe in; I would pray against fear
of losing faith in the things that I do believe in;
there would be no cold nights in the desert, no beads
of perspiration, nor the black beads of the Rosary
held as dried seeds between my fingers to ease pain
—no, Greek worry beads would be my choice,
one simple, straight-backed wicker chair, and a small
marble top table at some taverna in the shady village
square, or harbourside café on an island in the
Cyclades—and there, prayers that are not prayers,
for the things I have lost faith in, or fear losing,
would issue from the mouth's temple up into that
liquid light, formless as breath, and these prayers that
have no name, nor name any god, would simply
celebrate themselves in an act of soundless wonder.

Advice to a poet

Don't take the whole business too seriously. Adopt long distance walking as a hobby. Don't become a typographical cowboy or you will be mistaken for a signwriter. Guard against becoming a funambulist sans balancing pole. Failure means you are one step away from becoming a successful copywriter. Success means you are one step closer to never having to write another lousy word.

Advice to a playwright

Invite all those detestable people in your circle to first night. After the show abruptly leave *alone* by taxi for the nearest nightclub. This will prepare you for the morning review notices. Structure your dialogue as you would a scaffold: vocal pictographs around an imagined community of individuals. Discard long monologues about the world gone to hell. All people want to do is get home safely. The more *avant-garde* your play the better; audiences love nostalgia. Acts are for the apostles.

Advice to an English lecturer

Your future lies in the private sector. Stage dinner parties for book reviewers. Court publishers as your *intermediate* friends. Start up a literary magazine with an East European bias and nominate yourself as a cultural commissar. This is your birthright. Push post-structuralist theory through other writers. *Culture = Power = Exclusivity.* You are a cultural supremacist whose root cause is self-loathing in the knowledge you lack originality. Join the local Press Club.

Open-Learning Workshops / *afternoon*

Advice to a philologist

Converse with tramps. Record the patois of those who prefer to live under viaducts as opposed to living in stormwater drains. For a location guide consult your local government sponsored unemployment centre. Avoid detention camps. The language of the tin cup tapped out on bars in high security prisons is central to your understanding and visualising primitive speech patterns. Read George Borrow's *Lavengro*. Move into a housing estate.

Advice to a language poet

You have recurrent dreams of a ticker-tape parade on Wall Street. You are showered by your own *compositions*. Millions of letters and symbols. This dream symbolises your endless capacity to promulgate disinformation and untruth. The greater the abstraction the greater your success. Obscurantism equals originality which is, nevertheless, a borrowed concept. You are a social media terrorist and disciple of SoundCloud, Instagram, or whatever comes next. Infinity is a manageable excursus.

Advice to a book review editor

One day you will be taken seriously. Meantime, you remain the stooge of book barn syndicates. What author you promote will decide guest appearances at literary festivals, Hyatt Hotel book launches, etc. Safety lies in numbers. Affect an intellectual stance in the manner of a hipster film critic to secure regular, weekly spots on RNZ and Sunday morning TV talk shows. Join a gun club. Aim one day to become 'reviewer in residence' at a leading American creative writing school.

Open-Learning Workshops / *evening*

Advice to a literary festival director

You are, in essence, the grand puppeteer, politician of the highest bureaucratic order. You must be seen as the non-partisan dispenser of the public purse. Knights Templar of popular, *belles-lettres*. Spend your days and nights in the off season shifting through flowcharts and sales figures from multinational publishing companies in order to make a selection of authors. Beware the *margin call*.

Advice to a poetry society

You manage a glorified canteen for itinerant writers and a *trash & treasure* market for informal reading venues. As an amateur organisation that aspires to the trappings of the prestigious literary luncheon you are, at your most ambitious, nothing more than an imploding committee in search of a mediator. Your salvation lies in bus tours, to and from, retirement villages, and as a sideline, promoting *Poets in Parks*.

Advice to a young poet

Every thought is an act of translation; translation is the act of sympathetic betrayal. Poetry is the embodiment of memory and truthful record pays homage to it. The literary critic is the foreign agent in the camp. His job is to encode untruth and misinformation. He boasts theoretical abstraction and passes it off as informed judgement. He is in league with the fashionable clique of the day. Know this, and secure faith in your own poetic instincts—if for no other reason than to capture one elusive, revelatory moment.

THE LOST GERMAN GIRL

Berlin is desolate as a ruined beehive,
rows of hollow cells, avenues of piled rubble.
The slow exodus of refugees pulling small
carts a child might own, handfuls of scavenged
items. Where are they going, and in which
direction are they headed? Streets that are the
imprint of streets, spaces that once were
town squares, eddies of dust where fountains
played. Women in straggling lines pass
from hand to hand broken bits of belongings
retrieved from the rubble.

                    The lost German girl
listlessly walks a country road near the Czech
border. She wears rough trousers with
loose hanging braces, a black woollen top.
Her face, still beautiful, is bruised.
She puts a hand to her brow and hangs her
head in this short film footage—passes
out of sight forever to an unnamed destination.
The country road and green fields emptied now.

In the mouth of May another girl sits by
a broken wall in Berlin, stockinged legs drawn up,
her head resting upon her knees, and hair
fallen, too, like a shield, as if to protect.
Into what bright year will these two disappear?
One about to leave Berlin, a ruined dream
and dead nightmare, and the lost German girl,
expelled from Prague. They both exist
between these two purgatorial states, in that
No Man's Land, caught between loss
and despair, in the month of May, 1945.

DISSENTIENT

1.

      Three sparrows, moving toward
the same branch, on the same tree, create an
arrowhead. This is the discovery of
the projectile through avian flight; each
revelation has its value—this going back,
anonymously. Each city has its gravitational
pull (it's where you come from) rural
is always in the remembering; within the
present, slung back behind. You count them
along the backcountry road—twelve
poplars lining some rough driveway up to an
unseen farmstead. I mark them out as the twelve
apostles; a chorus of green candles in
spring that shed yellow through autumn.

2.

      Wind mercurial as Mary Magdalene
disturbs the combed-out soil of one ploughed
paddock. Limestone cave become grotto.
Mary had fled to Provence, gnostic
embodiment of wisdom, divine and fallible.
Cult and myth precipitated ritual, revered
earth as Holy Grail; deepened to sense of place,
light glazed landscape—rich as mosaic,
broken or brown as pottery placed at
the cave's mouth. Herakleitos said, 'The sun is
one foot wide,' that all the stars couldn't
dispel the night without the sun, that lightning
is everything, that consciousness has no
boundary, is fathomless in every direction.
Air must have appeared as crystalline to him.

4.

   Brain-shaped Antarctica. Now stick
a flag up at the South Pole for what you take as
dead centre. Let the huskies hyperventilate.
You come from another life, from the
backstreets and back stairs of an earlier era.
In this ice sheeted world life is a precious gem.
But at this precise moment your mind
is whiteout—thought a snow blizzard at sea.
From that flagpole of an indeterminate
life you rapidly recede vertically—observe,
sketched across your inner eye, that the
shape of Antarctica resembles a battered bicycle
wheel, whose buckled spokes all lead back
to where you are now standing, oblivious.

7.

   Rivers are reflections that pass
under mirrors of the curved, black night,
still and cold. Silence—is a hymn to silence,
spilled from the phylactery of the rounded
sky, stars out across the desert floor,
off the mountain ridge, bulking up behind,
rich coinage of the night, but this is
not Mount Pispir. Air so pure, it is tasteless,
and the sweetest air of all. He breathes
deeply, exhalation is the anima of
this desert place, he the locus of prayer
within it, his faith refuge and shelter against
demons who visit only occasionally now,
rising as wraiths off the rocks at midnight.

STREETS OF KIEV

after Osip Mandelstam

In Red Square, giant plasma screens loom blank
and wall-eyed, there's no news today. The Kremlin

thug needs time to think. He never counts his
losses, pays no heed to them. His mongoloid eyes

turn unperturbedly to the southwest. Any day now,
he will perform the prisyadka in Khreshchatyk Street.

Under the black belt moon, he cocks one leg,
a kick to the solar plexus, to the groin, to the temple.

Pectorals flex, abs ripple. His favourite cocktail,
Polonium-210, he serves up to those who dare oppose.

His expression resembles that of a firing squad,
this former KGB analyst calculates the odds quiet

as frost at midnight, his every move accounted for:
pieces of tibia, femur, cranium, each precious object

finds a place on his chessboard. Any day now,
he will perform the prisyadka in Andreevsky Spusk.

Prisyadka: *the squat-and-kick move that belongs*
to the Ukrainian 'Cossack Dance' known as Kazatsky.

SILENT AS A LANTERN

Flame is cupola. See it erupt from
shock-blown window frames of tall buildings.

      Boisterous as applause
exploding from theatre galleries. Observe flame's
upward curve, elegant as the carved prows
of Portuguese caravels.

      Blackened, rectangular
buildings, hollowing before uplifted crests of flame.

Imprisoned within this vortex,
colour bends to whitened heat—oxygen sucked
from the bellicose furnace.

      Flame over distance is voyage, prophecy.
Death throes of military campaigns;
otherwise, and always near, armies command it.

When campfires died, they marched, and flame
gripped cathedrals by the throat in a wreckage of light.

Sails dissolved into cloudbank, the false sunset
of cannon fire flickered, went out, silent as a lantern.

Whole cities became ash for archaeologists.

•

Flame is siren. Gérard de Nerval,
strolling the Palais-Royal Gardens, his pet lobster tied
with a pale blue ribbon.

Gargoyles danced prettily on the ramparts
of Notre Dame for him.

One of the poets known as *les bousingos* who came
together in riotous company over
potent rum punches, and ice creams served in skulls—

Théophile Dondey, who 'wore glasses in his sleep
so that he might see his dreams'.

Borel, 'with his feline teeth,
melancholy eyes fixed on the spaniel at his feet'.
Lilac scented beard, the mouth, an exotic flower.

On one black and white night, Gérard de Nerval
hanged himself in the Rue de la Vieille-Lanterne
from a sewer grating with an old apron cord;

he saw it as the Queen of Sheba's thigh garter—
a few scribbled notes on *Aurélia* found in his pocket.

He sought the 'eternal feminine' in the Lebanon,
Istanbul and Cairo, fled the black sun of melancholia.

'At times he lived gaily as starlings.'

IMPRESS

'and always that special slouch
as if leaning toward another, better, planet,"
        —Adam Zagajewski

They speak in the language of a landscape
that has vanished, before them and behind them.
They know the words carry an unfamiliar
echo in this land though, insistently, the song
stays familiar, much in the way some valued thing
lost will always remain familiar, the guarded
ruin of memory, familial; the sand drifts that buried
the village, the orchard auctioned off to investors
and chopped down; those remnants held over
from the olive press of sunsets still entraps them.
But this is the new land, and they must forget
in order to rebuild, to believe once again, even
if remembering is only the impress of fingertips on
a clay tablet. What is it then makes us distrust
the laughter in the voice? Big or small, recollection
is an ornamental dagger encrusted with precious
stones placed on display, always within view,
though never within reach, a ritual object laid out
in its glass cabinet, ghostly, yet intensely still.

THE JOURNEY

for Nicole Sprague

Decades of writing, unacknowledged, did not trouble him. A crafts-man. He lived an ordinary life in order to keep his extraordinary mind intact. The family grown and gone. Forty years a merchant on Brooklyn Heights. The business his father started. Sold every variety of antique clock, wall and column, black mantel and kitchen clocks.

Here, time whispered in hushed tones. His wife dead these past five years. An aloneness that announced an end to things. After all this time he finally completed one book of small lyrics.

He locked up his brownstone apartment. With a trunk full of newly printed books, poems that explored the minutiae of light and shadow over clock faces, those small mirrors of divination, he set out by Amtrak to crisscross every State in the Union. For as long as it took to empty the trunk of books.

Sought out libraries in cities and country places—journeyed across open prairies and mountains to find them. Peaceful work done at a leisurely pace. With a knapsack full of books he entered each library and, casually, walked by check out. No one paid him any attention.

An old man with cloth cap and knapsack. Found the poetry section, slid onto the shelf one copy of his book, correctly placed in alpha-betical order, then left as quietly and purposefully as he came. All across America. Then he went back to the brownstone, unac-knowledged, and died.

THE SONG OF GLOBULE: 80 SONNETS

1. *escape from Eden*

We could not leave the garden, we only
dreamed sin, and so we came to believe it.
One tumescent red apple brought us grief.
Old snake sidled through the night like a thief.
Cough. Slough. Was the ancient coat an ill fit?
She bought it, though knew he was a phony.
A stroppy full moon throttled the garden;
trees with no names danced amongst waterfalls
and glistened, way before the fall, shadows
gathered in sooty flocks amongst meadows.
God stomped and snorted in heavenly halls,
'I condemn them to life without pardon.'

Did Globule sprout seraphic wings for flight?
not beneath this bumpy sky—not tonight.

3. *bad boys & grungy bars*

A sun bungee jumped the hours of the day
over the back fence of her North Shore home.
The city shone bright as a bracelet 'cross
the harbour's makeshift waves of fairy floss.
She niggled and nudged at her comfort zone,
the harbour bridge arched, a grey bird of prey.
Her chartered accountant father (poor sod)
and her smiley, house-proud, aproned mother,
took it for granted she would marry the
boy next door—or next door to him, maybe—
did not doubt the books balanced her future,
but she fancied that dude with the hot rod.

She'd take City Rail to the Inner West,
Newtown bad boys and grungy bars, the best!

4.   southerly buster

A truck axle up-ended and upright
in a cloud collision stands Centre Point,
slapped up poster proud over the city,
battered, buffeted, lightning struck—ugly;
brassy as the town it's meant to anoint,
would be missed if it vanished overnight;
—fifty-six cables anchor the Tower—
which, if tied one to another, would reach
all the way from Sydney to Alice Springs.
As wind in the rigging of a ship sings,
would those cables twang along city streets
in a wind stretched, southerly buster hour?

Under this giant crow's nest in the food hall,
munching on a big burger, sat Globule.

6.   'mirror, mirror on the wall'

Famous for Nothing like Paris Hilton.
(No thanks) could anything ever phase her
in this prankster life that fled down the days
of her endless youth? Often, she did gaze
into the bathroom mirror's drippy blur,
hoping for—some sort of revelation—
(not likely) the word meant one fat zero.
A face stared back impassive. Goat-grey eyes,
half-surprised at, whatever, nothing much.
Her face, friendly as—in the mirror's clutch,
hungered for a grip on life, love and lies.
Just one more girl in search of some hero.

She sat on the stoop by the old wood shed,
then painted her toenails a fire truck red.

9. *siren song*

Fort Denison's Martello Tower sat
squat upon its rock, in middle harbour.
Handfuls of sudsy cloud drifted piecemeal
above the bridge, a half-sunk waterwheel
that churned the lazy day bluely over.
Out west, dully sounded a thunder clap.
Her friend Jade was only a tweet away;
the town sang its eternal siren song—
of that seductive choir she played her part,
swayed to the rhythm of the city's heart.
While the brassy sun beat its summer gong
golden bodies shimmered in every bay.

A bus to Bondi (the weather said fine),
though first she must wax her bikini line.

14. *burst like an aerial shell*

Globule celebrated fireworks as planned
glissading fan-like off the harbour bridge.
Puffballs of leery light *whizz! crackle! pop!*
Away from the CBD crowds atop
Bay View Crescent, she found a grassy ridge
to see the town turn into Disneyland.
The sky rained down bits of colour pell-mell,
Rozelle Bay blurred to a painter's palette.
Nearby, a party roared amidst the blare
of traffic horns welcoming in New Year.
She'd stay sober just for the hell of it,
meanwhile, sky-burst like an aerial shell.

City bells tolled as the midnight hour struck,
whole galaxies swirled in one clusterfuck.

17.   *more a hard grind*

Hanging close by the Coronation Hall
with the Subud dudes doing what they do,
some kind of weird meditation, she thought.
The windows of the Courthouse Hotel caught
sunlight in baubles (she had had a few),
as warbled patterns formed on the pub wall.
City Rail scraped out of Newtown Station,
a Boeing scuffed off suburban rooftops
so low you could read Dunlop on the tyres,
its fuselage scribbled on by church spires.
Here in the Inner West she'd learned her chops,
though more a hard grind than revelation.

The Subud dudes were kicking up a storm,
an old codger placed a bet, checked the form.

18.   *Sydney's oldest bones*

Watering hole for the local cop shop,
a pack of them claimed one end of the bar.
One bent copper's just as bent as the next,
stolid, stony-faced, stupidly perplexed.
A better pub than most around by far;
was Globule's occasional schooner stop.
Then, maybe, Camperdown Cemetery,
strolling by the giant Moreton Bay Fig
of St. Stephen's Church, historic tombstones,
resting place for the city's oldest bones.
She'd find some shady spot to light a cig—
within this walled enclosure's greenery.

A sandstone angel on a stele blew
his trumpet into the whisp'ring bamboo.

19. *ceiling fans susurrated*

Ku-ring-gai Chase National Park in flame
over the Hawkesbury, the horizon
jumped up orange under ember attack.
Ash blanketed Hornsby Shire, furnace black,
out across the Inner West postal zone—
the cops claimed an arsonist was to blame.
The public bar TV flared siren red
with regular updates from the fire front,
ceiling fans susurrated—folk sipped beer,
one feigned interest, others didn't care;
the locals played pool, a few took a punt,
or stalwartly played at pokies, instead.

The jukebox rasped with a leathery throat,
'she gone with the man in the long black coat.'

20. *primal gardens*

Dreams devolved into a nocturnal sport,
as if something else, or other called out—
'for where the mind is there is the treasure'
something beyond all value or measure,
though what did it mean, what was this about?
You might say she had little to report.
Or could it be that Mary Magdalene
walked the primal gardens of her vision,
this shadow figure, a few seated men
gathered under a palm by some sheep pen.
Tattered cloud at dusk in soft collision,
words she imparted received with disdain.

Yet deep within Globule's murkiest dreams,
Lilith whispered, 'All is not what it seems.'

26.   *Headlands Hotel*

Disorientation. Which path to take?
She considered east and west, north or south;
magnetic compass faltered, thoughts turned fog,
migratory birds through 'electro-smog.'
Her best option by far seemed word-of-mouth,
glossy package deals, she dismissed as fake.
The family packed up off to Thirroul
for Christmas holidays on the south coast;
but those memories lay drowned in sea mist.
The Headlands Hotel where she first got pissed,
the surfers and barbies, the Sunday roast—
that mad New Year when she near lost it all …

Coal carriers—troubling the horizon,
black and massive, the line lifted, broken.

32.   *Hellenic Bakery*

Down Illawarra then by Wemyss Street,
across Addison and Sydenham Road,
past brick villas with Dahlia gardens
(the first settled Greeks and Italians)
across the iron railway bridge she strode
munching an Hellenic Bakery treat.
As clouds built big airy tents overhead
she passed by a butcher and barber shop,
stepping over many a trachyte kerb.
Globule cut across Marrickville suburb—
at the cycleway she came to a stop,
so veered off to the Cooks River instead.

The river crawled under a pumice sky,
a bunch of office joggers bounced on by.

33. *takes all sorts*

Wasn't her idea of New York City—
crossdressers, ladyboys, traps, transvestites,
hustling blowjobs down on 12th Avenue.
Dudes traveling across from Jersey through
the Lincoln Tunnel for sex, boogie nights
in the Meatpacking District of Chelsea.
But hey, the Big City, it takes all sorts;
Sydney is no slouch when it comes to sleaze,
it teaches a girl how to pick her mark;
nailing some suit—just a walk in the park.
It's no easy thing for women to please,
to put on a game face, and be good sports.

We give thanks to the city's soothsayers,
cabbies, concierges, and bartenders.

37. *nereid of the waves*

Interlocking mortise and tenon cloud:
steadily, that sky unscrolls its blueprint—
she, the companion to light, shape-shifter,
dreams herself as waterspout and twister
dancing up the harbour in merriment,
who sways louchely as a watery shroud.
Undine or sprite—nereid of the waves,
a woman who would suffocate a man,
capture his breath with a kiss if betrayed;
does true love exist beyond getting laid?
One night stands—no, she was never a fan,
though, occasionally, one misbehaves.

Sydney girls, obsessed with real estate,
ensnare your man, get your house, renovate!

41.   crimson bruise

Victoria State ablaze with bushfires,
destruction along the Great Ocean Road;
Separation Creek, Wye River, houses,
properties, livestock—cinders and ashes;
the Otway Ranges ready to implode …
street after street reduced to smoking pyres.
This is the Australian bushfire season:
'today's expected high will reach forty'
as sunsets expand in a crimson bruise
from the Blue Mountains out to La Perouse.
Flaming pennants, an advancing army,
every state braced against the invasion.

Sitting on a balcony in Newtown,
around her sooty embers fluttered down.

42.   Olympia Milk Bar

Walking by the Olympia Milk Bar
(over there the Stanmore Cinema stood),
interior a dark, chthonic grotto—
everything faded like an old photo,
little survives of the old neighbourhood;
Mr Fotiou lives here, the Greek owner.
'50s advert signs drearily displayed:
'ice cream sodas' and 'time for a Kit Kat.'
Bold gold letters, 'Olympia Salon,'
'style cutting' and 'perms' a faded icon.
He dreams of Lemnos, but didn't go back;
of boyhood, and girls dancing in a glade.

A skateboarder clatters by, traffic hums,
Mr Fotiou sweeps his floor, no one comes.

45. *Mount Athos*

So she sat frozen before the portrait
in the gallery, grotesque as it was,
the painting looked at her, and she at it,
a frame of reference, the perfect fit;
Germaine Greer sculpted onto Mount Athos,
a ball-breaking, post-feminist piss-take.
One hand clenched tight in salute as a fist,
the other cupped the City of Sydney.
Allegory, island of the mind, farce,
Mount Athos trembled under the great arse.
Her face as blank as a monastery,
a monstrous dildo tethered to the wrist.

A thought floated up inside Globule's head,
'how can you be desperate if you're dead.'

47. *so long*

Probert St, the most burgled in Sydney,
or was, according to local folklore;
pot plants got stolen if not bolted down.
The cheapest rentals to be had in town,
an old working-class suburb, but no more—
why lament the loss of what used to be?
A photo's a dream you've departed from,
become memory, a faded address.
Joy soon wanes, dissolves into sentiment;
empty as any condemned tenement.
Bustling birdsong in volumes evanesce
down dusty country roads calling, so long.

Would she become a Mullumbimby chick,
bouncing some baby on her floral hip?

50. *hillock of her hip*

Aside from the yellow lit daffodils,
just weather, with a furrow on its brow.
If living is an act of postponement,
youth is the dream, the eternal moment
Globule resided in the here and now,
a handful of dreams, a few basic skills;
she saw herself living inside a cave.
The sun sank on the hillock of her hip;
O for a shack on a hill and sea view,
Illawarra escarpment running through.
To escape the city, take a train trip,
meanwhile, a surfer rode another wave.

Who would die of a broken heart today
given the temptations put in our way?

51. *loop*

She halted under the Iron Cove Bridge,
pigeons on girders clattered noisily.
She felt the *whump* of traffic overhead,
deep quad stretches, a sun flexed rusty red.
Globule tackled the bay run twice weekly
looping from Leichhardt back across the bridge.
Daylight lifted off the inner-harbour,
slid down between the sandstone abutments.
Shadow made of this a filtered grotto,
the moment captured, a smartphone foto.
Windows flashed off harbourside tenements,
traffic thickened—became an armada.

Jogged into Rozelle, hassled by some jerk
cruising in a chintzy, salmon pink Merc.

57. yet retain a hold

Crass Meriton development (Sydney)
nailing down the coffin lid on the old,
raddled jack hammers ringing neighbourhoods;
self-serviced apartments with all the goods.
Still, a few backstreets yet retain a hold,
terraces, villas, the bottlebrush tree…
Pocket handkerchief parks and squat brick walls,
balconies with ornate iron fretwork.
Refuse laden laneways and granny flats,
grey, wooden palings, ready to collapse—
the garrulous Greek and taciturn Turk,
the working-class pubs, the dim lit pool halls.

High walled presbytery, minus the Lord,
low plane roar over Chelmsford to Kingsford.

60. slow blur

Globule, trapped in a lift, talk about rude,
never read a book in his pointless life;
another Shane Warne dropkick sporting bling
who'd con some girl into a marriage ring,
a mouse-scared checkout chick born into strife
destined for this loser, this dumb arse dude.
Bragging to his even more stupid mate
about muscle cars, piss ups, backseat screws,
though his loud rant was directed at her.
Floor buttons counted down in a slow blur—
then she pushed past him muttering, 'excuse',
it felt like some weird dream and no escape.

Just another westie, yeehaw, redneck,
steel cap boots, navy singlet, trackies (check).

63. *hearts that harden*

She sat in the Warren View beer garden
beneath the frangipani tree—Ovid
on table, and of the many versions,
she settled on Clare Pollard's 'Heroines'.
Women writing warriors, she loved it,
read of hearts that bled and hearts that harden.
How Phyllis turned into an almond tree
that bloomed as her lover clasped it in grief;
or elms that grew from Protesilaus' tomb—
top leaves in sight of Troy withered in gloom.
Sitting there in the shade she felt relief,
emboldened even, though, somehow wary.

Once, it was looking ahead, now it's back,
had she now found herself on the right track?

66. *Briseis to Achilles / iii*

I write tearful words, I fear it's too late,
you handed me over to men the king
sent without so much as one farewell kiss.
Captive a second time, O my distress
at leaving—saw my family dying
by your hand, again, thus sealing my fate!
You sulk within your tent, refuse battle.
If Agamemnon offers you treasure,
tripods and gold, Lesbos girls, my return,
you hesitate, are slow to anger, spurn
all entreaties—is this your love's measure,
am I nothing more to you than chattel?

I never slept with the Mycenaean,
Achilles! My love defines who I am.

68. *Oenone to Paris / v*

So what if I slut-shamed whorish Helen,
for as you took her she took you from me.
By the sacred fountains of Mount Ida,
I warned you, do not hoist sail for Sparta,
even so, shipwrights felled the thick fir tree;
believe it, you are your own destruction.
Shepherd prince of noble birth wanting more
tossed me aside like some dirty dish rag,
for that rich bitch who ditched Menelaus;
chaos and death await you, I see this!
My love given is true, not like that slag—
you will return after wading through gore.

You beg me to heal your wounds, I will not,
far as I'm concerned, Paris, you can rot!

70. *Dido to Aeneas / vii*

Go, depart, the uncoupling sea calls you,
inconstant lover who beached on these shores.
I brought you to safety behind wide walls,
honoured your person in glittering halls.
Carthage stands strong against threatening wars
yet my brother in Tyre wants me dead too.
As waves roll you forward on the long sea
and your wife's ghost guides you to the Tiber,
there to found a city upon its banks
and build a great army in serried ranks,
know me for the one who will remember;
recall then my touch, both faint and ghostly.

Aeneas, your fleet rides in the roadstead,
one last time you rough-handled me to bed.

77. *Hypermnestra to Lynceus / xiv*

Forty-nine brides each guilty of murder,
that I held back, refused to slash your throat
was my crime—I disobeyed Danaus—
our wedding night, greasy smoke of torches;
a feast of meat and wine designed to bloat,
lull the grooms into a drunken stupor.
Three times I raised my blade over your head,
the dagger traced your throat, no! I could not.
Debated with self, but did not kill you;
your brothers' dying screams I heard, it's true.
I woke you, fiercely whispered of the plot,
'brothers, all dead, Lynceus—flee!' I said.

Here I languish, prone on the prison floor,
my wrists are shackled, I can write no more.

80. *follow the rails*

Chasing recollections, atmospherics,
labyrinths of the mind, sudden and fleet,
those utopias that will not be found.
The hum in the head that emits no sound,
parallel lines in space that never meet.
Globule was done with city hysterics,
she'd decided to strike out for the coast ...
travel north for awhile, follow the rails.
Waiting on the platform down at Central
she recalled her last trip to Newcastle—
coal carriers lined up, bulky as whales,
one pelican, hanging, pale as a ghost.

Someone's radio exhaled an old song,
'the last train out of Sydney's almost gone.'

CRANIAL BUNKER

PALIMPSEST

You arrive in Paris in 1902, as did Rilke,
age 26: great cities are the sum of all that will
happen to them, and like the weather,
omnipresent, that which will occur has, and the
past retreats into the future; clouds clog
the horizon, rise to vast, domed cupola upon
which you can project your own slide show;
the comings and goings, incidents unfold into
histories, the invading forces through the Arc de
Triomphe; Celan tumbles into the Seine,
Gérard de Nerval hangs from the grille 'in the
darkest street he could find', La Rue de la
Vieille-Lanterne; the myriad blank canvases ranged
along the Left Bank, like an endless procession
of days, waiting to be painted, to remake
Paris over and over. It is true, 'great cities are the
sum of all that will happen to them', palimpsest
of memory, that is little more than filtered
twilight; the child rings his bell, the red balloon
floats over mansard rooftops, '*where narrow streets
bend proudly to the stars*' [1] past the splayed,
iron petticoats of the Eiffel Tower; past & present,
an espalier of metaphor, woven through this
City of Lights, these blown banners of the ages.

          History is a slaughterhouse
preserved as museum. O it is Easter in downtown
Warsaw, and the Poles are whooping it
up nearby, consciously oblivious of the ghetto's
plea bargaining with the Lord, cries that
become silent film footage, flickering in the corpse
light. Hear how guilt congeals to anger

and accusation decades hence. We are heroes.
We are victims, book-ended between East and West.
We rode our horses against the German tanks,
'my rifle, my saddle, and me'. 'We suffered
countless incursions across our borders.'
Olga Tokarczuk, courageous, prized open the lid
of National Pride, to expose the hypocrisy.
'Slave-owners. Colonizers. Murderers of Jews',
only to have the ghouls turn, maliciously, against her.
History is a mass grave weighted down by
Public Monuments, a shroud stitched through with
anthems along the appliqué of Nationalism.
The shuffling steps of the refugees haunt their day
dreams. And finally, when dream has defeated
memory, it is safe to come out and stare at the rain
shiny curb; the brick walls weighty with a
mediaeval pageant of light, sodden, that blocks out
the heavy steps of the slowly dissolving armies.

A shunted siding of words brought to a halt
with an expletive, or begun with one. All those
light-fuelled days of remembered warmth
gone, dull as varnish. 'I want two bodies, one face
down one belly up', shouts the director, 'use the
fat extras'. He's a gung ho, hell yeah!
sort of guy, this is a Gulf War movie, 'they'll look
bloated,' he says. A movie shot down Louisiana
way amongst the cottonwoods and bayou.
He leans on an old tree trunk, sees a horse's head
in the bark. He makes a mental note that every
foreign conflict his country wages is a subconscious
rerun of the American Civil War. Night has
fallen back at the trailer, the movie's going nowhere
fast, but the plasma screen comes to the rescue.
The Eiffel Tower looms black as an obelisk
in the night, the lights of Paris dimmed to campfires,
flickering spasms of pain, the staggered glow.

Men in black tactical gear, the arrondissement
in lockdown. Bodies, the rubble-strewn restaurant.
Shot, she survived—only later to tell the media,
'*As I lay down in the blood of strangers …*' [2]
that she thought of all those she loved, drawing their
faces close round her, as she prayed, and bodies
fell, as finally gunfire ceased amidst the screams.

December 2015

[1] '*where narrow streets bend proudly to the stars*'—Hope Mirrlees / Paris
(1919)

[2] '*As I lay down in the blood of strangers …*'—Isobel Bowdery, Paris attack
survivor, Friday 13, November 2015

ARROWHEADS

That burning tree, the perfect touch
down into autumn, leaves, a high tensile
blue at dusk, buckling to orange;
tempered darkness struck through, the
living become memories of the dead.
Conjuring halls and bedchambers,
an age of saddle horses and war horses.
A yellow blade slants from one lit
window, elongates patio, bleeds shadow
darkly, as blue becomes an opaque
blanket rising into night. Autumn exposes,
once again, nests from newly forgot
seasons, beneath those trees cut
with copper foil. Birds work the branch
networks, parcels of song swapped
in the half-light. Cloud pelts shaken out
before an inhaling moon, near full,
over leaves cast into a scattering of bent
arrowheads. The air chill, chugging
with bird call. A dull, clapperboard sound,
wind gusts, rain hitting trees, that
far off fugue on Orini Downs—from
Maungakawa Reserve, a stitched, tree skin
cloak flung over Maungatautari, seams
thick along its flank. Windbreaks, copses,
falling away in an orderly fashion
out across the Hauraki Plains—squat
bungalows, crouched into the hills behind,
overlooking cloud and light flooded
lowlands. Back here in suburbia,
a half-submerged skylight, one sunken
moon, air slate grey as roof tiles.
Come morning, I will make my escape
from box canyon, head South on the
Waikato Expressway, skirt Cambridge

with its genteel stud farms, country
estates, wind my way up Sanatorium Hill.
Some morning, when those heights
turn heavy sleeved and baggy with fog,
and rusted roofs redden to autumn.

There was always doubt that lay indestructible upon the horizon, distant and beautiful in its formlessness, that appeared to be slowly massing but gave no indication of immediate danger. Disturbed and silent as mime yet still too far away to engage us, for it seemed to be a living thing. We could not be certain either way but manned our stations regardless although no order had been given.

The captain remained in his cabin poring over charts. We knew then that cloud had filled the sails, that the horizon had advanced upon us before we knew it, the deck still firm as any foundation beneath our feet, lifting slightly against the crosswinds that carried a sound open to interpretation. A low vibration diminished and faded soon as we felt it. No one could be sure anything had occurred.

There was neither a sense of impending danger nor anticipation only uncertainty. Each man stranded on the leeward side of thought. Each poised at the threshold of his shipmate's imaginings that verged upon revelation but this diminished also. Such was the unknown latitude of our arrested state and collective awareness. The one thing we suspected and later agreed upon was that all shared in this, unknowingly. Some lustrous cloud expanded above the rigging but just as quickly dissipated and was gone. Later, we tried to shrug this off and make light of it. The sea up to its old tricks again, confabulating stories. Even in daylight when the impossible only made its presence felt at night.

Compression of car tyres over wet cobblestones at 3AM. Otherwise, dead silence. One street lamplight bore witness. Two car doors cushioned shut. Then the splintering of wood, flashlights, the barking of orders, a scuffle and muffled cries. A cuffed, hooded figure dragged to the waiting 4WD, its engine thrumming. Acceleration. Once more silence descended as the night held its breath.

The poet stood in the dock. The dark suit given him appeared to be an ill-fit much in the manner of a clown. His head shaven yet clumps of hair remained. His expression stoic. One eye squinted intermittently; a bruise encircled it. Clearly, they had made some attempt to confine his vision. This gave him a discernibly startled look. The charges levelled against him were subversion, challenging the literary status quo. Non-compliance. His refusal to accept the terms of his contract invited ostracism and public ridicule.

Fear, that is, vaporised anger seeped through the hierarchical ranks of the literary establishment. The encrypted sentence dispatched from the Tribunal of Heretical Investigation instructed the provincial branches through the Federation of Subscribed Sycophants to deny him any access to official publishing houses within the state, ad infinitum. Banishment. An exile in his own land. But this was nothing new to him except that now it was passed into law.

It was observed during his mock trial that he was distracted though the accusations made against him demanded no response. Nevertheless, he seemed somewhat absent from the proceedings, and if his lips moved, he said nothing. His gaze fixed upon the ornate, wooden coat of arms on the panelling above the bench where his interlocutors sat staring down at him. But he did not see them. His eyes locked on that escutcheon of authority.

A snake coiled around a sword over a daisy chain of laughing children encircling the handle. A beam of yellow light emanating from the head of the snake like a death ray cut a trench around the children at the haft of the blade entrapping them, yet they were oblivious to this in their gay laughter. It was only years later that the samizdat surfaced. A memoir titled: *The Snake Trench and The*

Children. A lament for innocence defiled in the womb. There were reported sightings, but nothing confirmed. The poet had long since vanished.

FACTORY TOWN

       The suburb goes one way,
chimney smoke the other. One plane tree; its bole wide as
a well, lava flow of roots massing at the base,
next to the rusty rail line. A derelict munitions factory,
wall graffiti that reads, 'No certainties in this life'.

       Everything seems to be pushing away
from itself—clouds scroll Spanish like a rubric of skunks
on the move, clustering, only to expand and contract.

       Those brick facades
down main street, faded dull as dried blood, each with
its fugitive dank doorway, reeking of urine, or something worse.
There's no one to be seen, maybe the rapture had hit,
but this one orchestrated by neoliberalism.

       Nobody talks about the mayor's
speech he gave a few years back; the brouhaha it caused,
the boosterism, hand claps and backslaps—
turning the munitions factory into a 'museum/theme park,'
'revitalization of our abandoned factory town.'

       Someone talked about making a
documentary, but that never got done. Winter snows make
up for lack of heart, turning this place into some sort
of soft lens crime scene—from the helicopter's perspective,

seems peaceful enough down there, fairyland graveyard,
nicely packaged rust belt town. Trenchant as a death notice.

THE ARTIFICIAL FLOWER

I suppose one could say, she was surrounded
by a moat of admirers—the Polish beauty, alone
at her table in the Palais Kinsky, in Vienna,
May 1979. Her manner, languid, auburn haired,
it was her woollen dress drew me, large rectangles
chestnut in colour, like a fishing net, wide
as windows—was she naked, otherwise, through
those vacant squares; was this something contrived,
an illusion designed to ensnare? I can't recall.
A large flower head made up of some shiny fabric,
slightly brighter, it seemed, than her woollen
dress of loose rectangles, but part of it, blossomed
lavishly about her hips. She mesmerized me,
she and her dress, auburn hair, that artificial flower
in full, fabric bloom. I took the rose from the
small vase on my table, and walked across the
no-man's-land to where she sat, and presented her
with it, clumsily, I expect—unsurprised, she
turned her full gaze upon me, and what I felt was
paralysis; or maybe I appeared merely gauche,
unsophisticated to her, that is how it seemed.
I can't remember what was exchanged in the salon
at Palais Kinsky that night. A decadent party swam
about her. Someone plucked a champagne flute
from the waiter's platter, threw it back, then with a
bored, dismissive gesture, dropped it onto the
parquet floor with a satisfying smash, quite unaware
that he had done so, or had immediately lost
interest. No one else noticed. The Polish beauty
was already a closed chapter—perhaps she had been
absorbed into the frescoes on the high ceiling,
or become part of the Baroque clutter of the 17th
Century architecture? Wherever she went, she was
no doubt fully at ease, Countess of the Languid
Moment, such as her aristocratic forebears had

practiced and perfected centuries before, those who
still presided at the back of her mind in elegant
counterpoint. I was enthralled by her gaze,
captured by her insouciance, yet dared not cast one
glance toward that metallic, iridescent flower
that lay there, loosely burgeoning upon her thighs.

March 21, 2018

We broke up cobblestones, just as our forefathers had done, we the 'sans-dents' poor from the sticks, the 'great unwashed.' By the Arc de Triomphe we gathered, stood shoulder-to-shoulder with the 'gilets jaunes' (yellow vests) contingent; were fired upon with tear gas canisters, blasted with water cannon.

At the Champs-Élysées we faced off against police in their black riot gear, shields and rubber batons. For three days fought pitched battles, torched buildings, overturned cars. Some of us fell when we broke through the line, only to advance, and be repelled once more.

An exercise in attraction and repulsion, denial and acceptance, embrace and rejection. One body at war with itself, banners and clarion calls, alarums and flame, our bodies barricading one against the other as lovers do caught in the death struggle between love and hate, until exhaustion resolved the engagement.

Ancient battle cries that arose in the collective mind could barely be distinguished from our ferocious breathing—controlled these limbs in some grotesque pantomime. What we enacted would be preserved in memory, that dark hallway down through which time presses, relentlessly.

We observed the bridge between the wealthy and destitute slowly, inevitably collapse, the rich rose on one side of the chasm and the poor, the 'sans-dents' withdrew on the other. The day of conflagration had come, unavoidable and predestined. Each of those pieces of busted cobblestone we hurled in fury served as ostracon, and the casting of our vote.

THE MIGRATION

Weighty, full moon hoisting over ridge lines.
The flickering of torchlight, isolate, and forked lightning's
flared clematis, but this spelt primeval memory.

These revelations with us still, active,
though our minds had grown to eclipse them; slow
exchange from light into dark that birthed cave art.

       Reflection, momentarily, as torches
flickered through granular caverns; hush of charcoal passing
from fingertips—exhilaration yielding to song under
the moon as memory base.

       We saw death when light fell young,
spilling out over earth's threshold, that it was to our liking—
we tested fear to its limit, reproduced on a killing spree.

We were alive though shadowed by death,
this dissolved into a diminishing dream, half-remembered;
       the haunting of the self.

       Sunset, an anvil aglow in steady retreat,
rays fanning out, off cloud ridges making of them snow caps
but molten. An intensity of silence. Stars missile bright
coming in hard while the blurred negative of our Neolithic
selves materialized.

Every campfire a burning city, but that came later,
we trudged on, seeking difference. Forgiveness lay aeons
ahead. Yet none of us to blame, such a thing

could not exist—we felt no need to forgive ourselves.
The strong and the weak fell equally.
                    Throughout the migrations,
thunder ruminated amongst ravines, along mountain passes.

We met with 'the twang of the arrow, the snap of the bow.'
Our desires were for turmoil, not resolution. An eclipsed age.
                    Later, under full sail off the horizon,

either vortex or sextant decided our latitudes, shaped perspective.
Lampblack the sky shot through with star spittle;
                    Bronze Age before us meant the game was up.

Our demons shackled there where we wanted them—off
the bowsprit, nodding to the rise and fall of each foreign wave.

We were the blessed, the genesis, or so we thought,
though not the first, humanity came later. Others had arrived by
other routes—guided by the slow burning

                    of a collective mind, that glimmered
steadily before them, the gods' breath filling those sails,
chasing the wind—at least, how we recalled it;
we quelled ignorance, claimed everything that lay before us.

When first our hulls scraped beach gravel and sand
violence became a necessary act. Retribution soon followed,
and time began—then exhilaration gave way to fear.

                    Increasingly, barbarism met with barbarism,
we clave to the land, eventually outbuilt them, the shadow people.
'Your gods have forsaken you', we cried, 'your ancestors fled.'

                    Slate blue to the east, light blown to a ghost cone
out west. Half-moon scything across the valley. We tracked
estuary beyond salt marshes, pushed further inland until we reached

some rocky gorge and rested, built a cairn out of river boulder.
By that simple act—anchored ourselves to the territory,
                    the memory of this uncertain place.

Forest darkly folded over hilltops before and behind.
Wind lifted off river surface, elbowed through leafy branches;
birdsong, almost human in its strangeness, startled the men.

All around us that repetitive sense—presence retreating,
nostalgia for something continuously dissolving, irretrievable.

We lived in a time before boundaries confounded us.
Our minds belonged to the moment, endless. Anger we transmuted
into gods and birthed them, eternally castigated for this act.

                    Our lives caught between gravity and light
mirrored in conflict. Eden, the betrayal, served as apology by which
we conquered new worlds, over and over again.

After the expulsion, memory dulled, love an illusion born
of despair until finally, we found ourselves alone, upright and braced,
the long winter had begun—that loss, a forgotten treasure.

We defended ourselves against each other through our children
but to no avail. Rubble strewn memory angled into shadow and light,
made of itself a rose window.

Oak tree leaf, rusted haft of a Templar sword. Clouds laid out flat
as flagstones along the horizon. Bonfires arose to become cathedrals,
and footfalls sounded cataclysmic.

CHERT

Wolf howl of the chainsaw, intermittently,
river trending northwest to debouch at Port Waikato.
Cloud fashioned chert tool, another, spearhead
shaped. Buried light, deep shadow, blue dome intact.
Afternoon, winter encroaches, light glissades off
pittosporum demarcating the boundary line.

        Smoky light on paleo cave art,
her hair aglow, coppery as pine needles, there by
the river trail. Leafless, skeleton trees tilt riverward,
give onto Melville that claims the higher ground.
Backyard shed windows boarded up with plywood;
a broody suburb, predominately state houses.
Battle standards flag the sky, gradually, day bleeds
out into sunset. Traffic clots Cobham Drive.

Meanwhile, down by the river between bridges
and piers, hanging gardens—mapping coordinates.
Currents skirt an islet, angled afternoon light,
an electrum shudder expands, dims downstream.
Beneath the slide rule of traffic, rowing fours,
dragonflies under Victoria Bridge's iron shadow.

LADY OF THE MURALS

*'The memory of you keeps calling after me like a
rolling train'*—Bob Dylan & Sam Shepard/Brownsville Girl

Out of a headstrong cloud column emerged one square-rigged ship, buckled to the waves … But here the story neither begins nor ends. 'The entire landscape, graveyard, public gardens, Peacocke farmstead over the river, extensively undermined by rabbits,' you answered in response to her query about the innumerable burrows, and promptly imagined the whole shebang catacombed with intersections and way stations, a veritable metro subway system stretching for leagues— Kingdom of the Rabbit.

That smile O how it illuminated her calm, Byzantine beauty. Lady of the Murals. This Russian student, newly arrived to complete her Masters in Mesmerisation. You talked easily for an hour or so then parted. She pointed out that her name, Katerina, had Greek origins, 'like the Orthodox Church', she explained. Looking back, across to that trig station in the afternoon light, you observed within its framework a broad, tree-lined boulevard. Dusk, and headlights shimmering off into some other century, already dissolved in space-time, seemingly vanished through the wormhole. She truly present in the continuum that you had intercepted.

Before finally walking away you had already taken those farewell steps in your mind, embraced all you perceived of her in that sustained, shared moment. Departure can be understood as symbolic acknowledgement, an inverted greeting yet barely sensed, become footnote to this manufactured recollection. A brief encounter. Beneath the congealed sunset you tracked back to your car, strategically positioned for an unhurried exit, parked there amongst the memorial plaques and headstones.

Just another day of dames slamming doors. Downtown LA Bunker Hill. Once a choice place to live, now a place for those with no choice. Fire traps and dirty tenements. He'd hard-questioned the rare coin dealer who didn't know his time was up. The Western Union telegram waiting for him back at his Hollywood office bluntly stated, 'Services no longer required.'

The wealthy family who hired him to find the stolen Brasher Doubloon lay behind the theft, blackmail and homicides. The body count mounted daily and barely a week on the job. The client's secretary, deranged, terrified of the matriarch, had already fallen for Marlowe and his snap brim trilby. She held the answers as he held her. The temperature dropped before the rain did, then warmed again.

Harbourside city and shot put weather. The living are memories of the dead and dream is the four-poster bed of *Ars Poetica*. Call it by its real name. *The Takedown*. 'O the poverty of the boulevards!' slams in right on cue. Pick any slide show and add your favourite festival. Feels like waiting for either sermon or summons.

The day leaned back like some Robert Mitchum swagger. Any hedge is a maze in waiting, he reasoned. No leads, nothing you could poke a night stick at anyways. A lowering, crumpled tarp of cloud darkened. One slate slab on a blue backdrop. He recalled how Mulholland Dam's curve reminded him of an eyeball though with lopsided, monocular vision. Spillway leaky as a tear duct running from it. He saw the occluded shape at distance in sharp focus under pressure.

DON'T BE ALARMED

Banksy on his balcony at The Walled Off
Hotel imploding the barrier a leap away,
watchtowers left and right. The Israeli land
grab barricade winding off out of sight;
they play it systematic, and with stealth.
He sees it otherwise, maps his grid, memory
coordinates, seals up busted holes with
plaster to stop the darkness seeping through.

Silence before the rumour. A carriage
of thunder rolled away, cannon fire heard
in a cloud bank. Then the recoil, as
everything slipped back into place, millennia
hence. Don't be alarmed. Whatever befalls,
you are pitched, once again, into the chasm.
The millennial shuffle. Ploughshare moon
on a lopsided sky. Let the church bells toll
sublime from the primal arsenal.

Antediluvian breath, the twelve tribes
seeking the unattainable. Not your typical,
postmenopausal suburban scene, saved by the
flowerpot and watering can. The bullet hole
he paints on concrete glistens bright as crystal,
'The Scar of Bethlehem', over Palestine, too.
A woman heard at distance undeniably
emphatic, even in warbled laughter—
and poetry the articulation of forgetfulness.

The Medusa head burst from Taal Volcano,
Luzon Island, crackling with lightning
and godly invective, fourteen miles out from
Manila, as if some giant steam engine
thundered by under the mantle billowing ash
and smoke on track along the Pacific Rim
of Fire.

       American dream, the shredded
coat of David. So much for multiplicity.
'Used to be if you were a hard luck kid in
a dead-end town in a fly over state you learned
to play guitar or drums.' 'At least along the
way something instead of nothing.' Elizabeth
Wurtzel reads from her book, *Creatocracy*
at the Strand. 'Lament for a way of life that's
lost, for all that will no longer be,' swings
through the carnage of American pop culture.
'Money explains everything.'

'The Eagles sound like cocaine going
up someone's nose.' She pauses, sips from
bottled water. 'Money is where the action
is.' 'The teenager is gone, the lineal link
between childhood and responsibility.'
'Gone, just like the record album,' she says,
'love requires serious moonlight.'

'We are here to be entertained
and not do a Google search.' Lizzie reads,
'we are here to have fun.' Speeds through the
wreckage, hoping to outrun the black dog
of depression, addiction, suicidal love.
The lamp of hope swings way in the distance,
beyond and unattainable. False hope lies
within easy reach. Elizabeth Wurtzel. I.M.

DISTANT

'A mass of brass/
That sea looks, blazing underneath!'
　　　—Robert Browning

Bartender at the Pirate Bar, Hydra, moved
rhythmically to the 'Sultans Of Swing' nightly.
'His song,' you said, Greek girl from Alexandria,
the first to complicitly use me on that island;
how many others had you also? Your walls blankly
white (estranged artist parents, you told me),
were your eyes blank, too, or simply resigned?

I returned to that bar, offended, berated you
who listened sadly, said nothing, took me to your
bed a second time back in 1979. O stranger still,
your distant anonymity. All of us are tremulously
damaged, only admit to it with yearning bodies,
rarely our hearts. Loneliness, constant lover, patrols
borders of rejection, haunts us yet, down through
the wilderness of years—is that what you felt?

Even guesswork is inspiration if we trust it,
allow ourselves to balance on the precipice of
momentary belief, the possible, that awaits
as safety net below.

       Magpies, sharp as blades, move
across pine needles, light turning on its shield.
Did you hear the exaggerated rush of air
through branches? This is the falling, reversed
back to that step before you took it;
preface to a forest. Afterwards, a small breeze
by which leaves played piano keys.

       For the monk in his cell, play
of shadow upon the mat. See how he embraces
his God, whose arms, flung wide, make
an amphitheatre, and he at the centre of it, lifted
into the acoustic of his prayer. He recalls the
ancient dress code; sacrifice—art before religion,
memory before art. His cell a cave, as candle
flame danced, shadows applauded.

It was then he knew the still point, pushed
by deep silence, the shouldered, coastal hills,
darkening; though, it was the moon's
tabloid that billboarded the waves' ragged
italic, and halted him as he heard.

ANTHONY KINGSMILL-LUNN (1926-1993)

with thanks to Ann Diamond, fellow Hydriot

I am old enough now to talk with ghosts—they draw closer. Beyond the scent of thyme, you saw through pretension, painter of the Soho School, took me under your wing. You drank me under the table, one tin cup of Retsina after another on Hydra, refuge for painters and poets, musicians. You invited me back to your villa, fifteen minutes from port along the coast to Kamini, at the top of the gully. Your partner at the time, so much younger, silent mostly, wan, a Pre-Raphaelite beauty, said to me, 'Watch this.' As she prodded you out of your drunken stupor. How you growled and snapped awake. Maybe a cruel party trick for houseguests, who can say? Brilliant, delicate painter, acrylics and watercolours, a disciple of Cézanne, who captured that silvery light, the glowing whitewashed villas, so long ago. You told me 'grey' was the most elusive colour in nature. Would you have observed that the underside of a leaf is cloud coloured?

And trust, too, where you trusted no one. An original, first edition of your friend the poet, George Barker, inscribed and signed, you lent me to read, which in your absence I returned via Bill's Bar where we often met, prior to my departure. A return to Athens, briefly, then the Magic Bus to Salzburg, thence on to Vienna to fall in love, but that road lay some weeks ahead. Every poem is a letter to the lost and abandoned, those guardians of memory, of pain and loss. Even then, I sensed I would salute you years hence, where your ghost lay in wait. Hydra, those women who would take you, and take you into them, meant a shared moment of nothingness, pleasure for its own sake without meaning. How distant it all seems now—a dream; failed expectations, evaporations. You would have embraced mediaeval science that saw 'vision as light "dwelling" in the eye.' I heard you had died in poverty (a clochard on the streets of Paris), in London, the summer of 1993. That City of Light where you once studied at the École de Paris, telling tales of your friendship with Leonard Cohen for money and drink—where was your friend then who might have come to your aid, though likely your pride would not have allowed it? Anthony, rest easy in whatever ring of moss that now encircles you. True artist, a man who accepted me on trust alone.

September 18, 2020

FIG TREE

Remembering Christina from Baden-Baden on Hydra

Nothing seemed significant about it;
but this appeared to me over and over again,
there set in a recess on the hillside off the track
leading up from the harbour cafés and shops on Hydra—
one fig tree, early winter, late November 1979.

I hold this as memory I carried
with me from an arched, Venetian stone bridge over
some small stream or ravine along the coast,
to where she resided; either coming back, or going
over that ancient bridge, late in the evening, with the
German girl, she clutching a bottle of Demestica,
as she stumbled, nearly tripped—

who read my mind as I read hers
later into the night. 'Now you have everything you
want,' she whispered to me.

The hum at the back of the head making of it an
amphitheatre for voices, echoes, oracles. I again recall
that fig tree, standing there by the track, on the
island of Hydra, the memory of my night with her,
yearningly recent, reverberating within me as I passed
the fig tree to where I had stayed amongst
the whitewashed villas high up on that mountainous
island—

witness to how my senses had
vibrated like the strings of a finely tuned lute at the
back of my head in one stilled, sensual moment,
as I paused and passed on by.

EPIGRAMS FOR THE DISENCHANTED

An Informal Survey

2.   Folk don't express emotion openly
these days because they can't trust themselves.

4.   Every poem is a letter to the lost and
abandoned, those guardians of memory.

5.   Minor poets are as carp to ponds—an
infestation.

10.   Definition of love: couples constantly
apologizing to each other.

12.   The world is round as a bullet hole—
and this galaxy our exit wound.

24.   When a woman puts her lights on full
beam to attract a man, it is simply self-defence.

36.   Relentless data bombardment is a
stun grenade thrown into the consciousness.

38.   What is memory but building upon your
own accumulative ruins.

49.   He was reincarnated twelve times before
he managed to write his own epitaph.

53.   O nothing shallow about her at all, she
was an exercise in speleology.

67.   The secret of women's allure is that beauty
supersedes sex.

71. A dictator can't release his hold on power;
it's synonymous with immortality.

79. If the universe expands, accelerates into
nothingness—can nothing exist?

100. There is no God. Only frantic imaginings
of Sci Fi. We are the gods.

108. The Beatles are basically Coronation
Street on speed.

115. With European women, it is not just
intellect, but cultural atmosphere as seduction.

131. The village idiot's smile was more a case
of parting the face on either side.

142. Ghosts that exist in our minds are just
as real as those that do not.

147. The grammatical archery of English
perception; Americans employ a slingshot approach.

150. Ego-obsessed, or solipsistic poetry
is nothing more than a tip-truck tumble of words.

157. Arrowheads were invented by man
through the study of birds in flight.

162. Global tension? The film industry
and the pulpit depend upon it.

192. Women demand to be desired in order to enact
the power of rejection.

204. Tomorrow doesn't exist. Live for the moment.
That's where the action is.

218. And then, Noah said, 'The Lord told me there
will be climate change.'

229. Some birds & bats emit calls
at a sonic frequency we can't hear. So does thought.

240. If the Roman Empire had not existed would the
Christ figure have prevailed?

250. There is absolutely no end to the universe.
It is just waiting for us to catch up.

257. In the Beginning was Lust. And Laughter
fell upon the face of the Earth.

UNWRITTEN

Mountains are the homeland of winter.
Cities are caves where we leave our memories,
materializing into holograms buzzing a
Neanderthal encampment.

                   Light that flicked (you)
ahead. Shadowy anger of an extinct hominin
species tracks us yet, reverberates from

the deep well of the unconscious, lost along
migratory paths—vistas subsumed to
algorithms of dreamscape, ritual and recall;
that very act of incision is a recording.

It is a long way back to that old laughter,
still fresh on those windless, hapless days, long
since buried, then recalled.

                   It is a long way back
to some beige-glazed roadside paddock, high
summer, and the far off bark of an unseen dog,
the heat, emptiness ahead and behind.

It is a long way to those spirits the darkness
calls forth, either expectantly, or uninvited, that
swim in airy currents about you or in stillness.

                   It is a long way back
to the poem which lurks, unwritten and fugitive,
slowly forming, urged through your mind,

that emerges as hooded figure on the dark
road—caught in the lantern glare of your gaze,
his form falling into focus, as you advanced.

SHUTTERS

after Tony Hoagland

She told me, after I paid by card, collected my bottle
of red from the liquor store door (Covid level 3 lockdown)

muffled through her mask, 'He said to me,' she confided
in mock surprise, 'You don't seem to do much here.'

To which she replied, 'You don't know the shit I have to
put up with.' If strung out she didn't show it.

    On the path outside the Bin Inn (and Post
Office) a guy sits and holds up a cardboard sign that pleads

for food and money, who then as quickly walks
away when a hooded woman appears and takes his place

in a coordinated, business arrangement to maximize
returns, a practised gesture of bargain basement begging.

    Thoughts bang shut like shutters in a high
wind, slide to neutral as you turn the key in the ignition

and head back to your solitary unit, toward the nest of
dysfunctional neighbours, their low life, freeloading lives.

   I cope with this by imagining them
as extras in a Federico Fellini movie, grotesque figures,

behind roped off barriers, gormless, scratching bodies, staring
gape-mouthed at the beautiful heroine whose incandescence

goads them to animal shrieks and grunts, before the trucks
herd them back into the grimy, smoke-filled ghettos.

This transports me out of the neighbourhood for a while,
assisted by the bottle of red now sunk to a low Plimsoll line.

The following day, around midmorning, I will seek out
a back road farmgate to lean on and converse with the clouds.

THE PRINTER

for John Denny

There is something military about letterpress machines. They sit stolid and grounded, quiet as field guns in the no-man's land of the imagination, tempered and trained to respond under the guiding hand of the printer. Type selected and balanced upon fingertips, set letter by letter, word by word.

Press of the lever on quality cream paper stock. Conclusive, repeated click of machinery wheels. It speaks its own language. Meanwhile, the world outside the printer's shed hums and computes its obscurantist algorithms, oblivious to the press and bite of type, page after page.

Spring unfolds, hand stitching leaves to trees. What is it heard here, felt within the breath of machinery steadfastly at work, but the concordant and forgotten dialogue of horse hooves and carts over cobbled ways, rain punctuating slate roofs, a distant bell ringer, the lighting of gas lamps.

But then there is the slightest, barely audible hush of paper sheets that grow and gather into a stack, an exhalation of the printing press, telling of creaking sails at the inlet, faint piano notes issuing from an upper room of some long-lost village manor, fingers turning the newly printed page—while elsewhere, in dingy attics, the proclaimed manifestos of poets, artists, revolutionaries.

A conversation with the self is always an
engagement with 'the other', the undisclosed
identity, its presence made evident by the
anonymity of the question, nascent as sense
before thought—never asked. 'To whom do I
address myself?' Perhaps this is the guide
leading us through the sensory terrain out of
childhood's enclosure. The gate shut behind,
and that which must not be remembered,
never will. We cannot know 'the other' ever,
because it is always ahead of us, indeterminate
steps, but always beyond reach, and when
we stop, so too this guardian or guide, that
reminds us we are on a grand tour, perhaps
uninvited yet somehow, or in part, belonging.
Travelling over suspected terrain, though
unfamiliar, which I suppose for that very
reason is endless, as we pursue those shadows
in passing, wondering what we have missed.

FAR OFF

Each circumstance differed in that a woman
you otherwise knew, maybe the same physical
person, though not the same as she seemed
at another location, in some far-off country, or
that you had shifted in or out, at some other
remove; she already become memory, so too
undoubtedly, you to her. But even here you
were not privy to the moment, nor wished to be.
Somehow, you had both removed yourselves
from each other into something as yet undefined
or undisclosed, not quite strangers yet, though
you could never be completely that, emotions
safeguarded within an anonymity by which
you came to identify each other, apart from
each other, a manufactured indifference devoid
of even passing sentiment. Small changes
inherited from each, the barest of recognitions,
beyond lingering sadness or desire recalled.
And the heart pulling back upon dismantled,
sunken memories, held within that chain locker.

DEAD RINGER

British stamps from between the wars,
suffused with the reds of dying sunsets, faded
greens of forgotten countryside, amber
light off oaken panels seen dissolving through
the decorous counties of *Foyle's War*;
royal blue (two toned, with black mudguards)
or coal red paintwork of period automobiles,
the stylish trilby, hardly as rakish as the Chicago
or New York variety, nor the wearer so brash.
This is, after all, genteel English behaviour
of the '40s. Murder most foul remains, if not a
mystery, nevertheless, an abrupt and brutal
act, the hinge, like the brass hinged office doors,
through which decisions pass, upon which
everything devolves. Nostalgia is the happy face
we put on to disguise the protocols of loss.
The street procession. The shaky litter. The plaster
saint that teeters toward the cathedral square,
and villagers ambling at a leisurely pace—
something of the moon in its death mask stare.

Yet, to walk in the 'empire of shadows'—
ancestor worship, schizophrenia, hallucination.
O you can't fake time. 'Suppose', 'suppose',
once was, Wyatt Earp, 'the town-taming Marshal'
original 'beat' who as a young man bore a
singular likeness to Rupert Brooke, dead ringer
(go figure). 'Hell on Wheels' shantytowns
sprung up—Tombstone in advance of the Union
Pacific Rail (Old West) where 'men of every shade
and character' worked the silver mines. Earp,
whorehouse bouncer, coach guard, turned lawman,
branded an outlaw (shunned) back on the trail,
reputation more or less intact, but the truth never

told, dogged him, 'old sins cast long shadows'
into his sunset years. Earp didn't get to set
the record straight when alive; 'suppose', 'suppose',
whispered to (wife) Josephine on his deathbed,
but mythmakers had the last word. The End.

SHE WATCHES

One solitary, Turkish woman, looking
out through the meshed, screen door of her
home, silhouette still, a tessellated mosaic.
She watches, menfolk dismantle dwellings,
saving what they can, lumber, windows,
support beams, house fittings.

      The Birecik Dam now completed
as the Euphrates slowly rises to flood
this village. She has lived here her whole
life, the children grown and married.
Memory darkens to shadow. She watches
what once was, now ruins, mud walls,
partitions, tumbling into the rising waters.

As though she had forgotten she was
once young, eyes light-filled as the night
sky, how love waited, but this could
not survive beyond innocence, her fabled
histories reduced to rubble—old age,
yearning for that which no longer exists.

TREMORS

With Jack Gilbert, living on Paros
or Santorini, it was the freedom to let go,
trust his reach, wherever it took him;
houses tumbling like white dice seaward.
A simple thing, the beauty in the space
he got to defeat emptiness. My memories
float as kites back to the Cyclades, lapis
lazuli waters. Here, lip-smacking tar,
summer hot, asphalt roads. Heat mirages
dissolving off into distances. Out of sight,
over the river bend, sunset is a sunken
shipwreck within this southern archipelago.
Somehow, the tide of old friendships had
retreated way back from the shoreline of
some other self, and the tremors not yet
felt, of its seismic return—the horizon
steadfast as a spirit level, reassuring in the
way stillness is, when not a warning.

An uprooted tree after the storm cordoned off resembles a crime scene. 150 mph wind gusts burgling branches. The harried, nor-east getaway. The suburb looking like a shattered bird's nest. The unseen roar all night long. Vision is a reminder, it is an urging.

One white painted statue of the Christ figure standing before the Catholic church, arms spread wide, raised in the manner of a conductor, orchestrating the cosmos, and a world eternally fallen.

The seemingly endless flow, a habit of living, the big and small concerns like wagons arranged in a circle about our prospects at any given moment. But all that vanished with the global virus, everyone masked like bandits. No one able to roam the planet freely any longer.

Protests and illegal encampments. Blockades. People lamenting the loss of luxuries once taken for granted. Things not needed considered essentials for comfort. Expediency. Short term demands governed by short term memory. Consumerism as entitlement. A mixed bag of contradictory wants. Banners and flag waving. Contagion of selfishness rebranded freedom.

He goes to one of his two river lookouts. This one by the heritage mansion with its turret. He looks down the bushy slope to the path visible between the greenery then over the river, myriad ripples of sunlight passing in stillness. He is never overly bothered—cars parked further on down the road where the kids leap off the pier. But here he is left alone mostly.

The patient river flow emptying his mind. The city beyond the bank on the other side unseen. He sees terraced apartments with glassed in decking. The one remaining old wooden building with its three, snug balconies sitting grandly just below the ridgeline. An invitation to solitude beyond reach.

LONG SINCE ENDED

Wake of a riverboat ribbons out shoreward on this
or any other day. Primordial forest beyond dreamscape,
long since perished, partially glimpsed, ghosted the
mind. Had he ever been in love, or merely longed
for it, adventure turned disastrous, two lives drowned
in the net's entanglement? Decides he should never
have come back to the familiar, or seen from a train
window across a new country for the first time, jolts
memory of what he cannot determine or give shape to,
lingers momentarily. He wonders if this was meant
for him, something other intercepted, headed elsewhere.
What are ghosts after all but unfinished sentences,
relationships gone bad, long since ended but neither
had the courage to admit it, the way ahead less certain,
more a holding pattern than the journey undertaken.

DUCK ISLAND

There is a small island one side of the river,
close in to the shore, back from the stone stepped
embankment. An elevated water pipe on pylons
runs through to the treatment plant up ahead.
A narrow sweep of river, stilled, reaches between
the shore and Duck Island. Seats facing up river
along the walkway to the public gardens, the
island seen middle distance. One scrappy bush
consuming about a third of it. Maybe islet might be
more exact. An elderly man sitting there alone
looking toward it. I say to him, 'Imagine camping
on that island overnight.' He responds quietly,
'The river would be black.' Then he gets up and
walks away. That one remark alone made of
him a painter or poet, silence deep within him.

A NOTE ABOUT THE AUTHOR

Stephen Oliver—Australasian poet of sixteen poetry collections, seven chapbooks, and one memoir. Travelled extensively. Signed on with the radio ship *The Voice of Peace 1540 kHz* broadcasting in the Mediterranean out of Jaffa, Israel in the late '70s. Free-lanced in Australia/New Zealand as *production voice, narrator, newsreader, radio producer, columnist, copy and feature writer, etc.* Lived in Australia for 20 years. Currently living in NZ. He has published widely in international literary journals. Long-time contributor of creative non-fiction and poems to *Antipodes: A Global Journal of Australian/New Zealand Literature.* Poems translated into German, Spanish, Chinese, and Russian. Represented in the following: *Writing To The Wire Anthology*, edited by Dan Disney and Kit Kelen, University of Western Australia Publishing 2016; *The Australian Prose Poem Anthology*, edited by Cassandra Atherton and Paul Hetherington, Melbourne University Press 2020; *Poetry New Zealand Yearbook*, edited by Tracy Slaughter, Massey University Press 2021.